HELPING YOUR CHILD WITH A PHYSICAL HEALTH CONDITION

A Self-Help Guide for Parents

Dr Mandy Bryon and Dr Penny Titman

ROBINSON

ROBINSON

First published in Great Britain in 2019 by Robinson

A CIP catalogue record for this book is available from the
British Library

ISBN: 978-1-47213-876-7

Designed and typeset by Initial Typesetting Services, Edinburgh
Printed and bound in Great Britain by CPI Group (UK),
Croydon CR0 4YY

Papers used by Robinson are from well-managed forests and
other responsible sources

Robinson
An imprint of
Little, Brown Book Group
Carmelite House
50 Victoria Embankment
London EC4Y 0DZ

An Hachette UK Company
www.hachette.co.uk

www.littlebrown.co.uk

We would like to thank all the children and families we have worked with over the years who have taught us so much.

We would also like to thank our own families for support and inspiration. Mandy's family: Andrew, George and Kate; and Penny's family: Stephen, Ed, Jonny and Adam.

And since this book is for parents, we would like to thank our own parents for all their love and support – Sylvia and Len, Ann and Peter.

Contents

Foreword

There are many parenting manuals on the self-help shelves but none of them are aimed at parents who have a child with a physical health condition. As psychologists at Great Ormond Street Hospital with combined experience of over forty years, we are aware that when parents receive a medical diagnosis for their child this can have an impact on themselves as parents and on the whole family. Many of the parents we see are confident and experienced, but nonetheless find they have difficulties from time to time when dealing with their sick child.

For a range of reasons – feeling their child needs more understanding, is more fragile, is unable to cope as well physically or intellectually, or feeling that they 'suffer enough already' – parents sometimes experience concerns about how to handle their children with a diagnosis of a physical health condition. Sometimes parents feel isolated because they have no friends going through the same thing and the self-help books and parenting magazines aren't written with them in mind. The idea of this book is to give parents of children with physical health conditions specific advice and tips on parenting, focusing on those areas that many parents in our experience find particularly challenging.

How to Use This Book

Throughout this book, we have focused on the sorts of issues that might arise when caring for a child with a long-term medical condition across all ages and stages of their development, from birth to about the age of eighteen. In the early stages, you as parents carry all the responsibility for understanding the medical condition, developing relationships with health professionals, obtaining treatments and administering them. As your child gets older, on the plus side they begin to be able to understand and co-operate more with their medical treatment; but conversely, that increased ability to understand means parents must face other potential difficulties.

We know that children and families can thrive despite coping with a physical illness and do learn to manage complex treatment regimes successfully, so we have included ideas for developing resilience in both your child and your family throughout the book. The goal is that you and your family don't merely cope, but actively thrive despite some of the events that come your way, because of the shared experience the illness can bring. Each chapter in this book covers a separate topic, although some of them do have overlapping themes. Therefore, it is possible to read the chapters independently, to refer to sections that are currently relevant to you as a parent.

We are often asked by parents, 'How will I explain this to my child?' or 'What does my child understand about this?' Parents are usually the ones who first receive the diagnosis of their child's health condition and often have to explain the diagnosis or the treatment requirements to their child and answer any questions they raise. Chapter 3 describes the ways in which children understand bodies, illnesses and treatments at different ages and gives some examples to help guide you as to how to explain things to your own child.

One of the most heart-breaking aspects of being a parent with a child who needs medical or surgical treatment is watching them in pain and discomfort, because of the illness or because of the treatments and procedures they have to receive. It is not surprising that children who receive regular and ongoing medical appointments and procedures can develop anxieties and phobias about their treatment or attending hospital. Chapter 4 includes plans and strategies to help you as parents support your children though these difficulties. We are aware that parents, too, sometimes have phobias and hospital-related fears themselves, so we also take a look at ways to help overcome these, so that you can then support your child.

We have included a chapter on managing behaviour, because all children sometimes behave in ways that cause their parents to feel exasperated. Children with long-term physical illnesses are not necessarily more challenging or better behaved than other children; in many ways they are the same, so their behaviour will challenge you as parents at times. Whatever your own style and beliefs about parenting – from the '*laissez-faire*' approach that children should be free to express themselves, to the 'hands-on' approach that they should be guided to behave within clear boundaries – when parents arefaced with a very clear treatment regime that they need to impose, and a two-year-old just says 'no', their patience will be stretched. So, depending on your child's temperament, at some stage you will find that your child will challenge your parenting routine, authority and confidence, whether this is during the 'terrible twos', or as a seven-year-old who has decided to try to push back, or as a teenager who 'can't be bothered'.

Almost all children with a long-term medical condition will have nutritional requirements that are different from those of well children. This might be directly connected with the medical condition – for example, due to a stomach or digestion problem – or this might be a concern indirectly – for example, when children need to eat a higher-than-average level of calories or have feeding restrictions. Whatever the reason for nutritional guidance, parents often feel anxiety around eating and their child's growth, and hospitals weigh and measure children at almost every visit. Many children who have grown up having their height and weight scrutinised become overly concerned with their diet and body shape. For this reason, feeding and eating difficulties are given particular attention in this book in Chapter 6. There is an identified risk that, as these children reach adolescence, they could develop disturbed eating behaviours and attitudes as well as body-image concerns, so this chapter includes how to monitor and manage this.

We want children with medical conditions to grow up with a high level of self-esteem and feel resilient despite their medical condition. However, their condition or treatment regime may mean they look different or have to do some things that are different from their siblings and friends. Sometimes the difference is visible, such as a physical trait or a scar, and sometimes it is less immediately obvious, but the child will become aware that the treatments they have to receive, or their diagnosis, reinforces a difference. It is important that children are supported to feel that this does not make them any less valuable than other children and it should not be a subject of fear, shame or discrimination. You as parents are very well placed to help them because your child will see the way you manage difference and learn from this.

Chapter 8 covers the common issues children and parents face at school, and strategies to help with these. All children deserve to receive an education that will help them achieve their potential. In our experience of working with parents who have a child diagnosed with a medical condition in their early life, entering nursery and then primary school can cause great anxiety. There is no doubt that parents worry that teachers will not be adequately supported to look after their child's health needs, and handing over responsibility in that way can be very difficult. There are a number of issues that can arise because of illness in childhood that can have an impact on a child's education: receiving treatment, catching up on missed lessons and informing friends of treatment needs and diagnosis. As some children will need additional learning support in school as a consequence of their medical condition, we also provide information and resources about the statutory support strategies for children with special educational needs.

For many of you, your child with a medical condition will not be your only child, so we have included a chapter about siblings. This covers issues for well siblings and also when you have more than one child with health needs. Well siblings can often feel left out or have to try even harder to get parental attention, but there are also some ways in which they benefit, too. Many well siblings develop great emotional awareness, demonstrate understanding and empathy, and also provide a source of normality that medicines and hospitals sometimes remove from the family. However, parents often struggle with how to do the right thing for all their children, appropriately sharing attention between their well children and the child or children with medical needs.

Adolescence is often described as the most challenging time for parents; it is often joked about and the subject of much comedy. Entering adolescence can be much more challenging for children with an illness, and for their parents and the healthcare team. Sometimes the condition itself poses new challenges in terms of medical management due to the onset of hormonal and physical changes. It is important that parents have an understanding of the physical and psychological changes that occur as part of adolescence in order to understand the impact of these on their own adolescent. This is usually a stage when there is an increased desire for independence, and parents have to support their child to take more responsibility for their treatments and managing their health. Some children may not welcome this increased responsibility and you may fear that they will start to miss important treatments and their health will deteriorate.

Adolescence is also a time of many transitions, and one that will have a significant impact for a child with a physical illness is the transition from paediatric to adult healthcare centres. If a particular team has cared for your child over many years, it is a big adjustment to hand over care to a different service at the same time as allowing your son or daughter to take on responsibility for their own care.

Over the time we have worked with children and their families with long-term health conditions, very sadly we have also known and cared for children who have died as a consequence of their condition. Although outcomes for many conditions have improved significantly over the years, there are still some conditions that cannot be treated or cured. Children's palliative and end-of-life care services have improved, and this has become a medical specialty in its own right. Children, parents and other family members in this situation need and deserve specialist help, support and guidance, and the National Institute of Clinical Excellence

(NICE) has recently published guidance on end-of-life care for infants, children and young people with recommendations for good practice in this area. We have included some advice related to managing a life-limiting condition – for example, talking to your child about death and dying in the chapter about their understanding of illness (Chapter 3) – and some further sources of information and support are listed in the Resources section at the end of this book.

Finally, we recognise that parents of children and teenagers with a long-term health condition give a tremendous amount of themselves, selflessly. Parenting is demanding and time-consuming and many parents of well children would be flabbergasted to know how much more you have to fit into your day while managing treatments and planning. So we end by thinking of you and your wellbeing, caring for yourself and your relationships. There are suggestions for practical support but, hopefully, we will also convince you as parents that it is important to ensure you keep your own needs on the agenda and that sometimes asking for help for yourself is the right thing to do.

We are aware that families come in all shapes and sizes and we know that there is no 'perfect' family structure that is necessary for children to develop to their full potential and be happy. We use case examples throughout this book to illustrate issues and recommended strategies that other parents have found helpful. These cases are based on real issues from children and families that we have seen over the years. We don't make assumptions about what a family should look like; we are aware that a family is still a family no matter how large or small or how it is arranged and, from our experience, the issues facing parents often seem to be very similar.

Further Help

We hope this book will help support you as parents with the challenging but very important task of caring for your child who has a medical condition or illness. There is also a Resources section at the end of the book with a list of some of the main websites that provide additional support and information so that you can look for more help online. If you do feel you need more support, it is usually best to talk about this with a member of the team which provides healthcare for your child, or with your child's GP. There are local services in all areas that provide psychological care for children and, in addition, there are often psychologists or other mental health professionals attached to medical teams or hospitals who work specifically with children with physical health conditions. There are also community services, often known as CAMHS (child and adolescent mental health services), which offer assessment and treatment for children and young people with mental health difficulties, and these teams are able to provide more intensive and specialist support when needed.

2

The Challenge of Parenting a Child with a Physical Health Condition

Diagnosis at Birth or in the First Few Months

Some health conditions are diagnosed pre-birth or are apparent at birth or soon after. In these situations, parents are alerted to the medical or physical issues with their baby very early on, often before they have had any chance to settle into normal family routines. If your child was diagnosed at or around the time of their birth, you may even have little physical contact with your baby if medical intervention or surgery is required.

Parents in this situation sometimes report a whole range of feelings:

- Uncertainty
- Pressure to explain complex information to family and friends

- Lack of control over their child

- Loss and grief at not being able to take their baby home

- Incompetence and lack of confidence

- Loneliness and isolation

- Fear and anxiety

- Sadness and depression

- Shock and disbelief

- Blame and guilt (especially with genetic conditions)

- Is my sick child healthy or is my healthy child sick?

- Anger

Parents sometimes also fear that they won't 'bond' with their child due to being physically separated from them. Depending on the severity of the condition, you may be in a constant state of fear that you may lose your baby or the diagnosis will mean you don't have the skills to manage the condition on discharge from hospital. Some parents spend a number of days, weeks or months in hospital. During this time, you will have had to learn how to be a parent within a hospital ward and this has been described as feeling like being in a 'goldfish bowl'. This is an unnatural environment and parents often behave in a very different way during this phase from how they would in their own home. For example, you might feel you cannot relax because expert professionals are watching and judging your abilities with your child. You might not feel able to play with your baby or sing songs or make silly noises as you naturally would in your own home.

While the baby is in hospital where he/she needs to be to get the right help, parents can feel peripheral to the medical team. However, this is not the case – parents will always be hugely significant in the care of their child as they can see the needs of their baby as a whole. Therefore, parents make a crucial contribution to the team in ensuring that all the needs of the child and family are considered, throughout any inpatient admission and in planning for discharge. Parents help to keep normality on the agenda because they have to think about what life will be like at home as well as thinking about all the usual things that have to happen in daily life for themselves, their new baby and any other children or family members.

Some medical conditions are diagnosed via the national newborn screening programme when blood is taken from the baby via a heel-prick test at six weeks of age. These conditions are screened for because they can cause a lot of harm if not picked up early, and there is a clear medical treatment plan available. In some cases, early medical intervention is lifesaving; in others, the treatment is essential to prevent serious problems occurring – for example, phenylketonuria (PKU) and cystic fibrosis (CF). This method of diagnosis is essential for the baby to begin treatment but is often devastating for parents as they will have had no clue that the child might have any medical needs at all, and their baby may have been thriving. It appears to be all the more distressing to be given a diagnosis in the absence of any symptoms. Parents can be enjoying their new baby when strangers contact them and effectively remove the rug from under their feet by delivering life-changing information.

In this early stage, parents often feel that the diagnosis has been like an assault and may then respond to the medical team as their 'attackers'. This can be problematic long term unless this is acknowledged as an acceptable part of the diagnostic process. Parents feel an overwhelming need to protect their child. When told their baby has a long-term, potentially life-threatening condition, it is quite natural for parents to feel angry with the professionals delivering the diagnosis and have doubts or disbelief that their baby has the condition or about the severity of the diagnosis. Over time this shifts, so the condition itself becomes the focus of their attention. This can be a productive goal, as parents are then performing an essential parental role by monitoring their child's health, providing medications and treatments, protecting them from any potential risks to their health and ensuring that they attend hospital appointments or admissions.

The timing and nature of diagnosis varies according to the condition. In some cases, the way in which the diagnosis is made has a particular impact on the family. Most health-care professionals have specific training and give special attention to the development of skills in communicating a diagnosis; it is traumatic to receive and traumatic to give.

It isn't possible to make bad news good, but the way in which it is communicated makes a big difference. Most of these long-term conditions are managed in hospitals with a team of experts who are very aware of the impact of the diagnosis. These teams often include specialist nurses, clinical psychologists and social workers whose job it is to support the parents and not just treat the child.

Later Diagnosis as a Result of Deteriorating Health

The majority of long-term health conditions are apparent in the early years due to the recurrence of symptoms impacting on the child's health. Other conditions (e.g., cancer or diabetes) may develop later and can be of sudden onset. In both these conditions, the child has been well for a period of time and developing normally. You will have had time to adjust to parenthood, get to know your child and develop normal family routines. Parents sometimes report that although a diagnosis is devastating, they feel a sense of validation in that they knew something was wrong with their child. The diagnosis can often offer clarity when there has been uncertainty and you can take some comfort in knowing the treatment plan and expected outcomes. Nevertheless, both parents and children may still have a long period of adjustment to a complex and painful treatment or surgical plan.

Hopes and Expectations for Your Child

In this book, we use the term 'physical health condition' in a broad sense, to include a wide range of medical diagnoses, genetic conditions and illnesses affecting children who require regular, often complicated treatments or specialised management. The physical health condition is long term, not a few days of being unwell, and therefore not something that all other parents have experienced or understand. It may be that the usual sources of support available – for example, other parents and friends – might not be able to understand and so parents often feel they are coping alone following the diagnosis of a physical health condition. These sorts of conditions range from those that are relatively common, though no less worrying, such as asthma (which occurs in 1 in 11 children), to rarer conditions, such as cerebral palsy (about 1 in 400 children) and cancer (about 1 in 500 children).

Most parents expect to have a healthy baby. So, when things don't go as expected either at birth, shortly afterwards, or at a later stage in childhood, it can hit you like a ton of bricks. When parents are told that their child has a significant health difficulty, they often use words like 'devastated', 'catastrophic', 'state of panic', 'unbelievable', 'world torn apart'. The diagnosis often hits so hard because it appears to change all their prior hopes, plans and expectations. The diagnosis is not just information about the child, but potentially removes many of their previously held dreams of parenting a child and what the child may become.

In our experience, this initial phase changes and parents do re-establish realistic hopes and expectations once again, but it takes some time and work, not least emotionally, to restore those balances. If this challenge to the natural hopes and expectations of parenting isn't acknowledged, parents are often left managing these feelings alone and in isolation. Many parents feel that no one understands what they are going through. Sometimes even closest friends and family are not capable of providing the support needed; it feels like they say and do all the wrong things, even if done with good intentions.

Impact of the Diagnosis for Parents

Following the diagnosis, your perceptions of your child, ability to cope, and confidence in being a good enough parent can take a hard knock and family functioning can go off track. Some parents say that they are very 'up and down', feeling on occasions like their world has come crashing down and at other times hopeful that they are doing OK and coping. Some couples say that their relationship is tested, possibly accusing each other of not being supportive or coping with emotions in different ways. Some parents say that they don't feel able to manage with routine daily tasks such as food shopping and laundry, instead feeling overwhelmed by the diagnosis and what it means for their child and family. This is a temporary state of affairs and the family can often quickly start to try to develop a new normality and begin to function again. Parents are resilient because it becomes apparent very quickly that their child needs them. The physical health condition may mean that you as parents have to develop a range of new skills and routines, but your child needs you to continue being a parent, so those hopes and expectations can be realised after all.

The Importance of How You View Your Child

It takes time for any parent to adjust to the diagnosis of a medical condition and requires continual readjustments and recalibrations, not just about knowledge of the medical condition and how it may impact on your child's health, but also about how you perceive and interact with your child. For example, do you see them as sick or limited in some way by their health or capabilities? Or do you see them as a child first and foremost with some additional needs and adjustments that have to be taken into account in order that they overcome any limitations? It is perfectly normal to seesaw between worries that the diagnosis will limit your child's opportunities, and feeling optimistic that they will achieve their ambitions, especially in the early days.

Importantly, the approach you take towards the impact of the physical health condition on your child will influence their beliefs about themselves and their condition. They will learn from you how to approach any challenges they experience and will benefit from the knowledge and skills you have gained. We know that some children and families can develop a very positive sense of self despite their health condition, and they are admired and respected by the professionals who work with them. So it is important that you do feel you can get the support and advice you need to help you with the task of caring for your child in order to enable them to take a positive approach themselves.

The Medical Team and Parents' Role

It has long been accepted that the best method of care provision for children with long-term medical conditions is via a team that includes a range of professionals, who all have expertise in a specific area, working together in a joined-up way to benefit from all of their individual skills and knowledge (i.e., a multidisciplinary approach). Traditionally, the core paediatric team consists of a paediatrician (a doctor specialising in working with children) a nurse specialist, and then health professionals from additional specialties, such as a dietician, physiotherapist, psychologist, pharmacist, occupational therapist, social worker and play specialists. Fully staffed and committed teams have the best chance of achieving high standards of care so the child is as well as can be.

Providing good-quality care relies on frequent monitoring, quick recognition and response to symptoms and preventative treatment. Sometimes admission to hospital is needed to provide more intensive or complex treatment when symptoms increase or complications develop. However, most of the time a child is cared for by their family at home, so much of the responsibility for this increasingly complex and vigilant management lies squarely on the shoulders of you as parents.

As has been noted already, parents are the hidden and sometimes unacknowledged members of the multidisciplinary team. The medical team often sees parents as one might view a patient, as the recipients of care. But they are not the patient; they are the 'go-between', the bridge between the child and the team. As the child gets older, they will also begin to have a say in their own care, and they will contribute more and more actively to any decisions that need to be made.

The health professional's duty of care can be best achieved as part of a model in which parents are explicitly included as a member of the treatment team. Parents should be included in the team, and it is important that they are given a full explanation of their child's condition and medical treatments, and the opportunity to express their views and preferences around their child's care. Parents, children and professionals should not be construed as 'us' and 'them', but as partners on the same side working together, with treatment of the health condition as the shared target. Parents need to feel included and they need to establish a mutually respectful relationship between themselves and the medical team. For such a relationship to be successful, there are rules of practice – everyone has a responsibility to make the partnership work. If the relationship is grounded in a framework of mutual trust, then it can both function and flourish.

Sometimes a parent's perspective can be challenging for health professionals, but the best response to such challenges is to work to maintain a relationship with parents. This can be done by understanding their perspective, developing mutual respect, and recognising that this may be a gradual process that takes time. In some rare cases, when doctors and parents cannot agree on the correct treatment or the benefit of treatment, and when this cannot be resolved between them, this might end in a law court. These situations do not happen very often, and are extremely difficult for all concerned, so it is important to maintain relationships with the team in order to ensure that any disagreements or concerns can be discussed openly and differences can be resolved within the team, whenever possible.

Key Points

- The time of diagnosis can be traumatic with parents experiencing a range of painful emotions.

- Whatever the age of the child at diagnosis, parents have to cope with changes to their hopes and expectations of themselves as parents and for their child.

- Medical teams include professionals trained in offering support such as clinical nurse specialists, psychologists and social workers – it is recommended that parents do take up offers of support as this can then help them support their child.

- Parents need to have access to support to help empower and create resilience in their child, reducing any negative impacts or limitations of the health condition.

- Your relationship as parents with the medical teams may become long term – it should be one that is collaborative and respectful.

3

Children's Understanding of Illness

Some of the frequent questions asked by parents are: 'What does my child understand about their diagnosis?' ... 'What can she understand at this age?' ... 'How do I tell her without causing her to worry?'

In this chapter, we explain the child's developing understanding of bodies, illness and medical treatment and give some examples of ways of talking to children about illness. There are no set ages at which children acquire understanding or knowledge, because it does depend so much on the individual child and their experience, but we do use age ranges to give an approximate guide for different levels of understanding.

Case Study – Kyle (6 years old)

Kyle has been admitted to hospital due to a serious chest infection and suspected pneumonia. He needs to have antibiotics directly through a vein (intravenously). This means he requires a catheter (long thin tube) inserted into his arm and the end of it is visible at the top of his arm.

Kyle has responded very well, and the medical team is very pleased with his progress. However, Kyle has been very withdrawn, unsettled and is crying a lot which his dad says is very unusual as he is normally a confident and lively boy. The nurse caring for him spent some time speaking to Kyle and, after getting to know him a bit, she asked about what he understood about being in hospital. Kyle knew he had a bad cough and was poorly but what he didn't understand was what was wrong with his arm and if he would ever be able to use it again.

Once the nurse explained to Kyle why he had a tube in his arm, even though his arm was fine, he started to relax and return to his old self.

Sometimes we forget that young children don't have the same ability to understand illness and medical treatment as we do as adults. Kyle was a bright six-year-old boy who understood and accepted that he needed medicine to help his chest get better. Kyle knew where his chest was but what he couldn't understand, and everyone had forgotten to explain, was what his arm had to do with it.

Children's Developing Understanding of Illness

Children can acquire quite sophisticated understanding even at quite a young age if they have had a lot of information about, or direct experience of, something. Children who have a lot of experience of illness, treatment, doctors, health professional, clinics, tests and hospitals will also potentially have expert knowledge of these things that seems to be beyond what would be expected for their age. However, there are a few general guidelines about children's level of understanding that can help guide how illness and treatment can be explained.

Young children

From about three to seven years of age, children understand their world from direct experience, copying and repeating. We say this is a 'concrete' understanding. This means children are very accepting of the things they see and are told, so if you tell them a ball is called a ball, then that is accepted. In young children, this is the word they will use initially only for that specific ball, but very quickly they will start to use that word for anything that looks like that ball.

As we get older, we develop the ability to think and consider information given to us and don't always take things at face value but, by and large, children under about the age of seven are very trusting. As a parent, you are likely to have a lot of influence over what your child knows and understands.

At this stage, the child understands the body in terms of what it looks like on the outside and understanding about the inside relate to what they put in it (food), what they can feel (bones) and what they can see come out of it (wee, poo and blood).

Daisy, age 5

Figure 1

They can understand that they have other things inside the body if you tell them, but they won't have a very good image of what it looks like. For example, in the illustration (Figure 1) drawn by a five-year-old child, there is little idea of exactly what is inside the body. The child has coloured in the arms and legs red to indicate blood because they have seen blood come from inside the body, and lots of lines indicating bones, because these can be felt from the outside. For Kyle, he understood that he has a chest and that he needed medicine for it, but he couldn't make the association between the medicine seemingly for his arm – for that is where it was put – and it making his chest better. So Kyle thought he had another problem with his arm.

Young children have limited ability to understand the concept of illness (see Figure 2). They can begin to make cause-and-effect associations; for example, if they fall and scrape their knee, it might bleed, they might need a plaster and then it gets better, the blood stops and eventually they see their knee looks like it always did. A young child might associate the knee getting back to normal with the plaster; you might have said to your child, 'Let's put a plaster on it to make it better.' You then might find that your child asks for plasters at lots of other times when you know a plaster won't help; for example, for a tummy ache or a bruise.

At this stage, children can think illness is caused by magic or as a punishment. A young child might hear their parent say, 'If you don't put your coat on, you will catch a cold.' For a young child who then gets a cold, they may think this is the punishment for not wearing the coat.

Figure 2 – *Understanding of Illness in Young Children*

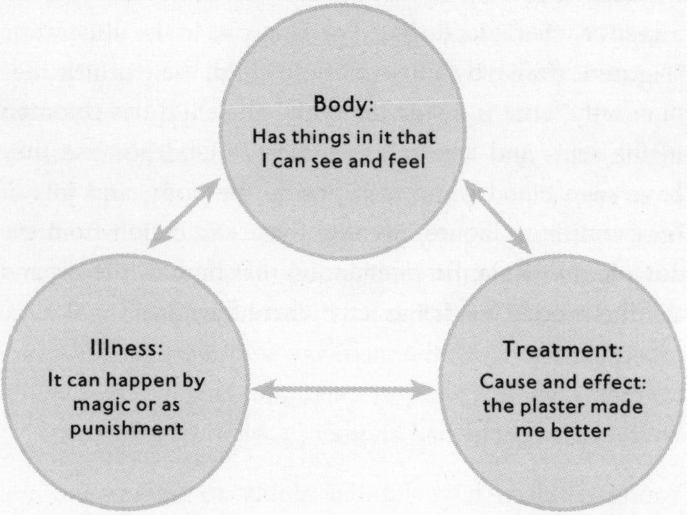

Body:
Has things in it that
I can see and feel

Illness:
It can happen by
magic or as
punishment

Treatment:
Cause and effect:
the plaster made
me better

Middle childhood

In the seven-to-eleven-year-old age group, not only has the brain been developing to enable better understanding of things, but your child will also have had more life experience, so may have acquired direct knowledge of their own body, illness or treatment, or acquired it from other friends or family, story books or television. While children in this age group typically have more sophisticated understanding than younger children, it is still not the same as adults. Children will now have an ability to understand more of what is inside the body and will have some understanding of how things connect. For example, when we breathe in, air goes into our lungs. They may even understand that we need oxygen to live and how this gets passed into the bloodstream. They will have a simple understanding of digestion, that what they eat comes out again after the body has taken the good things out of the food. But their understanding is still quite concrete; for example, most children at this stage assume that their heart is heart-shaped and, generally speaking, they accept what they are told by you. For example, in Figure 3 the eight-year-old child who drew this picture has an understanding of some of the organs inside the body but not exactly where they are.

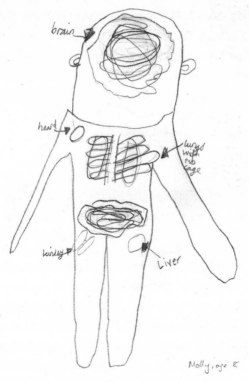

Figure 3

Children of this age are also developing an understanding not just of illness, but of being healthy. They can now understand the information they have been given about certain foods making them big and strong, and also that eating certain foods can have a bad outcome; for example, too much sugar can damage your teeth. Although they know and can repeat these statements, they might not quite know exactly what it means, unless they have had direct experience, such as needing a tooth filling.

Children are often told facts about their medical condition but don't fully understand it yet. For example, children might have been told that medicines help them digest their food, but actually don't know what 'digest' means or how the medicine helps with the digestion. Between the ages of seven and eleven children begin to understand what germs are and that these can make us ill. So, understanding of illness is not so much based on magical thinking but on a real understanding that sometimes illness happens because of germs being transmitted in the air or by touch. Children in this age group may begin to think that all illnesses are caused by contagion, caught from the air or from someone else, and it can be very difficult for children to understand that their body developed an illness by itself.

Explaining treatment to children in this age group still needs to be simple and straightforward as they are still only able to put together cause-and-effect associations: 'I got ill ... I took some medicine ... I got better.' They are not yet able to understand that they may need to take medicine to prevent them from becoming unwell, as some medical conditions require, or even that they feel well but then need to have treatment that makes them feel unwell (see Figure 4).

Figure 4 – *Understanding of Illness in Middle Childhood*

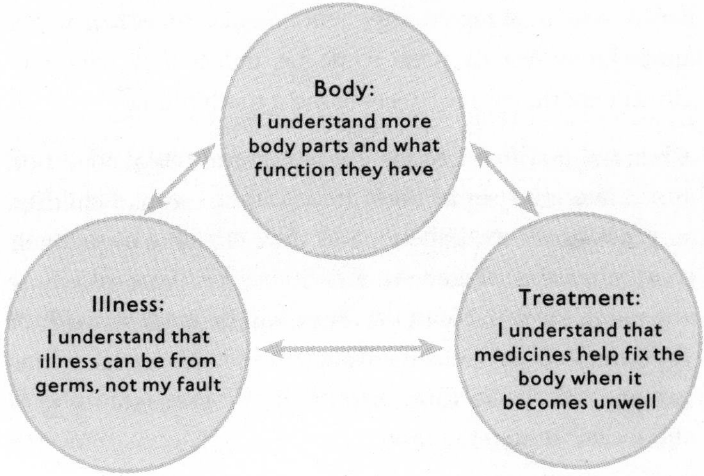

Body:
I understand more body parts and what function they have

Illness:
I understand that illness can be from germs, not my fault

Treatment:
I understand that medicines help fix the body when it becomes unwell

Older children and adolescents – 11 years and older

At this stage of development, children are typically getting a much more adult-like comprehension of bodies, illness and treatments. But it will vary greatly over this age range and it is important to bear in mind that full brain development is not complete until the mid-twenties (see Chapter 10 on adolescence). Children at this age can have a more adult-like discussion about illness and treatments; they can be included in some planning and decision-making about their own personal health needs. But note that they may not be ready for independence in managing health, illness or treatment needs. They still need support, particularly for complex decision-making or where there is a high level of uncertainty about the illness or treatment needed.

Children in this age group can understand how illness arises not just from germs but also from injury; they can appreciate changes to body functioning – e.g., acquiring an illness such as diabetes; and they can also have some comprehension of genetic inheritance of some diseases, such as sickle cell. However, there will be great individual variation in their understanding and so it is important that parents and the medical team do not make assumptions about their understanding.

This age group are also capable of more sophisticated understanding of treatments (see Figure 5). They can grasp that some treatments or behaviours are to prevent illness or keep the body healthy. They also understand that a state of mind can have an impact; i.e., emotions can affect the way in which you cope with an illness, manage the treatments, and that it is possible to have mental as well as physical illness.

Figure 5 – *Understanding of Illness in Older Children and Adolescents*

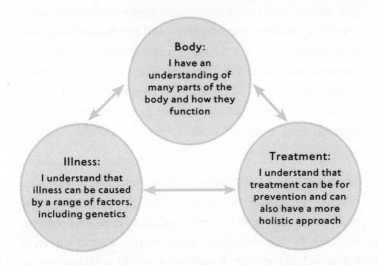

How Do I Talk to My Child about Their Illness?

The way you talk about your child's health condition as a family will impact on your child's approach to the illness. It will also affect any other children in the family, and other members of the extended family, too. Families have different ways of talking about difficult issues, but it is certainly true that trying to protect the rest of the family by keeping things hidden can be very stressful and it may prevent you as parents or other family members, such as siblings, from receiving the support that they need themselves.

A mother of a seven-year-old boy diagnosed with leukae-mia initially did not want to talk openly about her child's condition in order to protect him and the family. However, as she later explained, 'I had to run round like an idiot try-ing to snatch these conversations with the doctor without my son knowing . . . I didn't want him to know what was going on . . . I persuaded them not to talk to him. Having done all that, I carried it all by myself and that was the worst thing I could have done really.'

Before trying to explain the illness to your child and other people, make sure you fully understand what is going on. Then make sure you have had the time and support to begin to 'get your own head round it' and therefore begin to accept and understand what will happen to your child, your family and you. You need to get some strength yourself to be able to pass on that strength to your child.

Plan in advance

It is helpful if you can plan who will tell, when to tell, where to tell it and what to say. Deciding who will explain the illness and treatment to your child is very important as you know yourself and you know your child. If you think back to any occasion when you have had to have a serious chat with your child, who was best at it? There can be more than one person present but make sure that this doesn't make things more difficult to manage. Your own mum might be well meaning but is she going to interrupt and interfere? Or would you prefer it if one of the medical team did this?

When

Timing is important because if your child is old enough to know that something unusual is going on, then they are old enough to put some pieces together themselves. You need to get the balance right between getting yourself equipped with the right information and ensuring your child hasn't already become overly anxious because they have used their imagination to fill in the blanks. It is important to remember that the facts you give them could be far less worrying than the stories they have imagined in their heads. Usually, talking to your child is part of a process rather than a one-off event, so it can be helpful to let your child know that there will be a chance to come back to you with questions or worries they have thought about later on.

Where

The location is really important. For younger children, it should be a calm place, comfortable and, if possible, familiar with no distractions. A busy place with lots going on will mean they are easily distracted and find it harder to take in the information. For older children, you need to be aware that 'having a discussion' could cause tension and anxiety in itself. Sometimes it is best to raise difficult issues or give information during a shared activity, so you don't have to be face to face, for example, while sharing a task such as preparing some food or making the bed. This won't work for everyone, but for some the information is better given and received if it isn't made into a big deal (even if the content *is* a big deal).

What

It is sometimes best to get help with your script from the medical team. You can put it into your own words, but many parents feel more reassured if an expert has given them the words to say or helped them to think through what they might say. There is not one 'perfect' way of giving information, but you may feel more confident if you have had the chance to think through some of the options or wording you may use. It can also be helpful to start by checking your child's level of understanding and what they already know. Whatever you say and whatever the age of your child, information should be clear, concise and may need to be repeated. You don't have to say everything in one go: just give the amount of information needed at that time. It is helpful to think about just giving them enough information that they need to know at that time as you will have the opportunity to develop their understanding over time. For young children, avoid abstract or hypothetical ideas – use clear facts.

Sometimes it may seem easier to make it sound as though things might not happen in order not to frighten your child, but be careful if this is giving false information. You might be tempted to say something like, 'The doctors aren't completely sure, it might not be the case, but anyway you have to go into hospital, but don't worry about it.' This will have one sure-fire effect: to make your child worry! Also, you want your child to be able to trust that you will talk to them honestly, so if they find out you have been concealing something from them, this will make it much harder to believe what you say the next time.

It is always a good idea to check what your child has taken in. Asking your child to repeat back what you have said can be helpful; for example, 'So . . . what do you make of that – does it make sense to you? What is it I have just told you?'

Case Study – Yemi (12 years old)

Yemi is twelve years old and she has just been diagnosed with diabetes. Although she has felt unwell over recent weeks and is aware that she has had tests, she hasn't yet been told the diagnosis. Yemi's mum thinks it would be best if she tells Yemi rather than the doctor doing it. Yemi is a shy girl and the doctor is a man, which Yemi's mum thinks will make things worse, not better. Yemi's mum has spoken to the diabetes nurse specialist and has got all the information about the condition and also about how treatment will start and what will happen next for Yemi:

Mum: *Yemi, I have spoken to the doctor and he has got the test results. We know why you have been unwell.*

Yemi: *I'm busy, tell me later.*

Mum: *No, Yemi, this is important, you need to know, come and sit in here with me for a while.*

Yemi: *Oh my gosh, is it really bad, am I going to die?*

Mum: *No, come in here next to me, sit down and let me speak.*

Yemi: *OK, Mum, I'm listening.*

Mum: *You have what is called 'diabetes'. Have you ever heard of that?*

Yemi: *Yes, I think so. A girl in my year has it . . . I don't know her though.*

Mum: *It is quite common; there might be lots of kids at your school who have it.*

Yemi: *What is going to happen to me?*

Mum: *You are going to be OK . . . I have spoken to Sarah the nurse who knows all about diabetes and she is going to help both of us with starting your treatment.*

Yemi: *Treatment? What is that? I don't want treatment.*

Mum: *Medicine . . . you have to take medicine every day to keep you well.*

Yemi: *Every day for ever?*

Mum: *Part of your body that helps you manage your sugar levels isn't working so well. So the medicine you take does that job for you. You take your medicine and your body does the rest.*

Yemi: *What sort of medicine?*

Mum: *Well, the best way of getting this medicine is with an injection, but I know all about it, it isn't difficult and everyone gets used to doing it themselves after a while.*

Yemi: *Mum, I'm scared; I don't think I can do it.*

Mum: *Of course you can, come and give me a cuddle. Whatever it takes I will be there, we will get on with this together. The most important thing is that you will be well, and fit and healthy.*

Yemi: *What happens next?*

Mum: *We are going to see Sarah tomorrow. Do you remember what it is you have got?*

Yemi: *Diabetes, and I hate it.*

Mum: *I know it is hard [gives her a hug] but we will do this together. Have you got any questions? I might not know the answers but we can write them down together and ask Sarah tomorrow.*

In this example, Mum chose to do the telling herself and she found out as much as Yemi needed to know for now. She made sure she had Yemi's attention; she heard Yemi tell her she was upset and scared, but she was reassuring and got Yemi back on track. She gave Yemi physical contact, a hug, and verbal reassurance that they were in safe hands with Sarah and they would face it all together. She ended the discussion with something practical by writing down Yemi's questions. If you choose to write down questions, you may need to limit the number, just in case the questions start to raise anxiety. Just simply say, 'That will be enough for now . . . we can ask the others another time.'

Why me?

Many children, particularly older children, will say variations of: 'Why did this have to happen to me? It's not fair, I've got nothing to look forward to.' It is heart-breaking for parents to see their child in distress and they often feel helpless that they can't take the illness away. You have probably already had those thoughts yourself though, and know that you have to get through it for the sake of your child. You can't answer their 'Why me?' question but you can allow them to express their emotions and show you are supportive and willing to listen.

The next phase is to help your child adapt to living with their medical condition. This isn't a one-off event; it is a process that changes over time. They will need your help to:

- Deal with pain and symptoms

- Deal with hospital, clinics, tests and staff

- Maintain an emotional balance

- Preserve a positive self-image

- Preserve their relationship with family and friends

- Possibly prepare for an uncertain future

Younger children are likely to need your presence to give reassurance and security, and they are likely to need your physical contact. They will also need you to interpret what is going on because they will find it difficult to take on information directly. In middle childhood, children will watch and hear what is going on and may well pick up on verbal and non-verbal cues. They still need you to be with them, noticing how they are reacting, and taking care of them. They need you to be calm, patient and keep your own anxieties under control as far as possible. It is also common for children and young people to 'regress' or act and behave like a younger child when they are feeling under pressure, so you may find that you do have to adapt your approach to help them take on information.

Older children also need their parents as an ally, and although they may understand more about the condition and the treatment, they will need the opportunity to discuss the impact on them and their lifestyle. They may also try and protect you from their own worries and may therefore find it harder to be open with you about what concerns them. While they may not respond well to the suggestion of 'sitting down to talk through your worries', you will probably find that there are opportunities that come up every so often, sometimes when you are busy doing something together, when they feel more comfortable about talking about their concerns. Try and make the most of these times because it can be hard to create these opportunities at the time that suits you best.

Having Someone to Talk To

It is really important that you as the parent have someone to talk to about all this. It doesn't necessarily need to be someone from the medical team or a professional – it can be your partner or a friend, your own parent, your child's teacher, someone who you feel is listening and taking your feelings seriously. You need support to help your child adapt, so both of you can be positive about the future and tackle any difficulties that do come along. This should help you:

- Adapt to changes in your lives as a result of the illness.

- Be your child's buffer – you are their comforting shield–you can interpret the doctor's instructions, you can listen to your child's worries and can help them find the support they need.

- Develop and know your own coping strategies and make use of them when you need to. For example, if you cope best when you know what to expect from the appointment, you can agree with a nurse that you will always phone in advance to find out what is planned.

- Improve both your and your child's ability to communicate; practise asking questions of your child after their appointments: 'How did that go?' or 'Did you understand what the doctor said?'

- Help your child to get the skills to manage their own health condition.

- Maintain your child's good self-esteem and feeling that they are respected by praising them for their involvement; e.g., asking questions in the appointment, listening to their views and taking them into account so they feel they are included in managing their health condition.

There is more information about ways of caring for yourself and your relationships in the final chapter.

Talking about Life-limiting Conditions and Death

Fortunately for children with a long-term health condition, it is still rare for the condition to cause death during childhood, even if it is life-limiting. One of the hardest things to talk about with your child is the subject of death or dying, but if your child does have a life-limiting condition then this may be a topic that you will need to talk about at some point.

You may have some opportunity to discuss death at a time when it is not related to their own illness. Just as we discussed earlier in relation to understanding illness in general, a child's understanding of death and dying will depend on their experience, as well as their stage of development. Many children will have had experience of something or someone dying – for example, a pet or a grandparent – which will inform their understanding of death. However, we know that it is hard for children to take in all the different implications of death. For example, they may understand from seeing a pet die that it means their pet is not here any more, but they may find it hard to take in the finality of death and they may question where their pet has gone to. If you use these opportunities that are not related to their own illness to talk to your child about some of the issues raised by death, this will help to shape their understanding.

One of the reasons it is very hard for a parent to talk to their child about this topic is because of the level of distress that they feel themselves, and their own difficulty in thinking or talking about this possibility. It is therefore essential for you as a parent to draw on support for yourself, in order to be able to manage any conversations with your child. There are additional resources that you can find to help with this and some of these are listed in the Resources section at the end of the book.

Over recent years, children's palliative care services, including hospices, have expanded their services to offer a range of support strategies for all the family, but many parents still find that the thought of using these services is too upsetting and they do not want to 'give up' on active treatment for their child. Many fear that discussing or planning for the possibility of death is a form of 'giving up hope' that could result in their child or themselves giving up. However, these services have a lot of experience of managing life-limiting conditions and death in childhood and expertise in talking about options, so it is worth considering using them as it can be very reassuring to get support from professionals who have a lot of experience of this type of work. These services will usually offer the option for parents to visit without their child first, to discuss what is offered and to have a look round.

It may also be hard for you to know what to tell your child about what happens after death – and this will depend on your own beliefs. If you have a very strong faith of your own, you may be able to answer your child's questions based on your own beliefs. But many parents find that being in this situation is so difficult to manage it can challenge their pre-existing beliefs about life after death. Nonetheless, it can be very positive to talk to your own religious leader, as they will be familiar with the questions raised and can be a great support.

If you do not have a strong faith yourself, it is still worth talking through your own beliefs with someone, as it will then be easier to answer any questions your child may ask you about what happens after death. The same principle applies that it will be easier to talk to your child if you have also had a chance to prepare yourself beforehand, and even if you are not able to fully answer all their questions, you will feel more prepared.

Nowadays, if you wish, it is possible to include children in talking about possible death and help them to be involved, as well as their parents, in any choices about where they die; for example, at home or in a hospice or hospital. However, any of these discussions would initially be with you as a parent, so you would have the opportunity to get support for yourself first, as well as think about the extent to which your child can or should be involved in these discussions. Families have different views about these important issues, so it is essential that this is done in a collaborative and supportive way.

Developing Resilience in Your Child and in the Family

Developing resilience is a method of identifying ways of building up your child's skills in a proactive way in order to help them develop a positive outlook towards some of the challenges they may face as a result of their condition. We know that some children and families can develop a very positive sense of self and they are admired and respected by the professionals who work with them. While this approach can actually benefit all children, it is particularly helpful for children growing up with a long-term illness and a way of helping you to feel you have some positive strategies to handle any issues or difficulties that come up.

Over the last couple of decades, legislation has been passed that any form of discrimination is illegal. Policies are now focused on promoting inclusion, not exclusion. Psychologists working with children with physical health conditions have been very aware of discrimination, exclusion and difference as themes and the impact these have had on developing children's sense of self and confidence. (See Chapter 7 on managing difference for more details on how to deal with other people's reactions and building your child's self-esteem.)

Nowadays, it is potentially easier to enable any child with a physical health condition to grow up with a healthy self-image without perceiving themselves as unnecessarily limited by their health condition. We want to help children discover their potential and encourage resilience so that they set themselves goals and ambitions in the same way as their peers, despite their health needs.

You can encourage and build resilience by ensuring that you think about the words you use to describe your child's health condition; avoid negative-sounding phrases such as 'you have something wrong with you' or 'disease'. Try not to refer to treatments as being for 'illness', but more to keep your child fit and well. As a family, include your child in all the activities you would do anyway: just make adaptations. If your child's health condition means that they require a particular daily treatment – for example, physiotherapy – make it as fun as possible, and consider if anyone else can join in the exercises. Conversations about future achievements should be positive; focus on what can be done rather than limitations. Build confidence and feelings of competence in your child by:

- Praising their strengths

- Avoiding comparisons with siblings or other children

- Recognising and taking up opportunities to build on their strengths

- As a family, engaging in activities together, doing something that everyone can join in

- Including them in family chores with tasks they can achieve, as you would your other children

- Encouraging them to take an active part in decision-making

- Planning to adapt – accepting challenges and finding ways round them rather than ruling things out

---

Key Points

- Children's understanding of illness will gradually develop over time, and is influenced by both their developmental stage and their experience.

- Children will be influenced by the way you talk about their condition so it is important for you to have the time and support to understand their condition and treatment, and to be able to talk openly with your child and give as much information as they need to know.

- Under stress of illness or treatments, children can regress to earlier stages of thinking and coping. So even your teenagers may need you to speak on their behalf.

- Older children also need reassurance, particularly if the treatment is long term or uncertain, but may be more reluctant to discuss their feelings openly.

- Take any opportunity to discuss their condition and their fears when they feel ready to do so.

- Take a proactive approach and develop a sense of resilience in your child as well as the family as a whole.

4

Managing Anxiety around Medical Procedures and Hospitals

Procedure-related Distress and Anxiety

For many people, the thought of having any form of medical test or even going to a medical centre or hospital immediately brings on anxious feelings. Having to take your child to hospital for tests or treatment can fill you with horror. There are very good reasons why people develop anxiety or fears connected with medical tests and hospitals – it is because the experience has been painful, frightening or embarrassing in the past, and we don't want to repeat it.

Anxiety can cause any or all of the following:

- Sweating

- Feeling faint

- Butterflies in the stomach

- Racing heart

- Feeling sick

- Finding it hard to breathe

It is normal to experience anxiety when faced with a situation or object that causes fear. The anxiety we experience is a result of changes in our body caused by a chemical called adrenalin and, in some situations, this is a normal and helpful response. Adrenalin enables us to respond to a dangerous situation and is often known as the 'fight or flight' hormone. For example, in the past when faced with a physical threat, this enabled our ancestors to escape dangerous situations.

Sometimes we can experience high levels of anxiety even when the situation is not actually very dangerous – this may be because we have either experienced something unpleasant associated with it before, or because we have interpreted the situation as dangerous when it isn't. This can lead to a phobia – a fear that is not based on a real danger. Many phobias lead to strong feelings of anxiety just by thinking about the feared object; for example, some people feel anxious even when thinking about spiders. Many children will automatically get feelings of anxiety when told they have to go to hospital, even if a test isn't planned, and they will try to do all they can to avoid having to go – often by throwing a tantrum or becoming extremely upset or distressed or simply refusing to co-operate.

Often, even if the procedure itself is not very painful, the thoughts and feelings created in the build-up to the event can make the thought of it distressing. It is more often than not the memory of the whole event being unpleasant that causes us to become anxious rather than any actual pain from the procedure. This is called 'anticipatory anxiety', where we begin to experience anxiety before the event; often, the event itself is not as bad as we had convinced ourselves it was going to be. Quite often, children will try to avoid the procedure because of their anxiety, and well-meaning parents and staff end up getting caught up in endless negotiations and discussions of what might help, during which time the child will be growing more anxious.

As a responsible parent, you have to take your child to appointments and ensure they have their tests done in order to manage their heath condition. However, this causes an awful conflict for most parents as you want to ensure your child is well and gets better, but you also want to protect your child from pain and distress. There are a number of strategies that can be used to help your child by either preventing anxiety in the first place, minimising the anxiety associated with the procedure or managing anxiety arising during the course of the procedure. Case examples below help demonstrate how these strategies can work. You can try using these strategies yourself, but also hospitals often have play specialists who are trained to help your child prepare and manage hospital procedures.

Case Study – Shannon (7 years old)

Shannon has severe and complex asthma. She now needs to go to hospital once every five weeks and stay for the day in order to have treatment for her condition. Shannon is already wary of hospitals because she has been going regularly since she was very young. She has had X-rays, scans and her lung function measured many times. Mum has agreed with the doctor that Shannon needs this more intensive treatment, or her asthma could have serious consequences.

Shannon knows she has to go to the hospital clinic, but her mum has not yet told her what will happen. Mum is worried that if she gives too much information, Shannon will refuse to leave the house. On the day of the appointment, mum is highly anxious. Shannon is aware that mum is acting differently and is constantly asking her what is going to happen.

It is really important in Shannon's case that time is taken to help her mum feel calm in order to get Shannon to feel more relaxed before any procedure is done. This might mean that the schedule of the day takes longer but the risk is that if Shannon is too frightened, the procedure will have to be cancelled anyway. Have a look at the following recommended techniques to see how they might help you in your situation.

Talk to the medical team

Never be concerned about asking for time or someone to talk to in order to prepare for a procedure. Time spent preparing yourself and your child before a procedure is time well spent if it helps prevent treatments being cancelled or being carried out when your child is already very distressed. Patient satisfaction is an important outcome for hospitals, and nursing and medical staff would rather have a successful outcome and happy families than a complaint and distress.

If you have enough time before the event, it is worth talking to the nurse or whoever is doing the procedure so that you are clear about what is going to happen, and you have a plan to manage your child's anxiety. If you go into the situation feeling more supported and confident in yourself, this will benefit your child. There are also lots of resources online that you can use to help familiarise yourself and your child with medical procedures (see the Resources section at the end of the book). You may also be able to meet with a play specialist who is trained to help your child prepare and manage hospital procedures. Although it will help to familiarise your child and yourself with what is going to happen, it is sometimes not enough in itself to prevent anxiety, and you both may still need additional support during the procedure itself.

Distraction

This is found to work best in the early, anticipatory phase. You can use anything as a distraction technique, depending on the child's age and interests. Younger children can be distracted by moving objects and toys, whereas older children may find counting forwards and backwards can occupy their mind. More often than not these days the best form of distraction is electronic, such as a game or film being played on a phone or tablet. Distraction is a very powerful tool; it seems so simple, but it is very effective, and parents often think it is too easy to be true until they have experienced it working with their children. Just try to take note of how many times in a day your partner or your child gets so absorbed in something that they no longer even notice or hear you. Think of a time when you have said, 'No, we've lost him, you won't get a word from him now . . .'; for example, when the football results come on the television or the theme tune for their favourite programme starts. Distraction works because all the focus of the child's attention is on something else rather than on the feared procedure.

Breathing exercises

These are aimed at helping the child actively to learn mastery over anxiety rather than becoming passive and submissive. Breathing exercises can also help the child to divert attention away from the procedure because they are focusing their attention on something else. The procedure is best taught using modelling, with the child's parent also doing the exercises. It can help to use a visual image to encourage the child to engage in the breathing; for example, pretending that your lungs are like a balloon, and breathing in over a count of two to fill the balloon, then slowly breathing out over a count of four to make the air flow out again.

If their breathing has become faster because of anxiety, using the counting will actually help slow it down, and it should also help them to begin to relax.

Guided imagery

This is often used in conjunction with breathing exercises and the best imagery needs to be worked out prior to the procedure to fit in with the child's interests. It works by making use of the ability of children to use their imagination to create a vivid image which helps focus their attention away from the procedure and also enables them to relax more. For example, you can ask them about their favourite superhero, cartoon character, role model or film star. A story is then developed that includes the character using their powerful, special skills to help the child cope with the medical procedure. Older children and adults can produce their own fantasy image that is incompatible with pain; for example, a favourite place they like to go to where they feel calm and relaxed. The health professional or parent then prompts the child to use their imagery during the procedure.

Filmed modelling

A film is made of another child with the same medical condition undergoing a procedure. The film includes the health professional guiding the child through the procedures. The child in the film describes his/her thoughts and feelings and how they are using coping strategies to reduce their worries. There are many films of this sort available for routine procedures online and some of these are listed in the Resources section at the end of the book. This can be particularly effective because it also helps the child understand they are not the only one who has to undergo these procedures, and also demonstrates a way of mastering the worry created by the procedure itself.

Practice and reward

The child rehearses the events of the procedure beforehand, including the stages of the procedure, each coping strategy and how they might feel. They then undergo the procedure using their coping strategy; e.g., blowing bubbles or counting slowly. The child then receives praise and an agreed reward at the end of the procedure, usually a badge or certificate, although in the case of older children, the satisfaction of undergoing the treatment successfully is reward in itself.

Child practising being the coach and using positive coping statements

This strategy works well for young children and refers to the child pretending to be the nurse and to carry out the procedure on one of their toys. The child coaches the toy to use breathing exercises and distraction. At each stage, positive coping statements are made as observations of the toy's progress. So, your child might tell the toy what is happening, such as, 'First, I am going to wipe your arm with a wipe, then get my butterfly to look at your blood . . . very good, teddy, you are being very brave . . .' and so on throughout the procedure. Your child will benefit from this sort of technique if they are very familiar with a procedure that is frequently repeated; it also helps if they have a good imagination and are good at pretending. You are involved to describe and promote coping skills used by the toy (the toy is in place of your child, so you have to praise the toy as much as you would your child). This process is conducted on several occasions prior to the actual procedure; parents are then used to help coach the child at the event.

Case Study (cont'd) – Shannon (7 years old)

For Shannon, there was no time to arrange several preparation sessions prior to coming into hospital and so the best course of action was to help calm her anxieties and use distraction at the time of the procedure being done. The play specialist spent some time with Shannon to find out what sort of toys and activities interested her. Shannon accompanied the play specialist to her store to find some of the things she would like to take with her to the room. During this time, mum met with the nurses to find out exactly what would happen to Shannon, so they could work out what mum's role could be. Some parents choose not to be present; Shannon's mum wanted to be in the room and to sit close to Shannon, but out of the way. Mum was asked about her worries and concerns and was able to acknowledge that she was anxious and guilty that she hadn't been able to talk to Shannon about it.

Shannon returned to her room with an array of activities and arranged them in order of preference around the room. Mum told Shannon that she had met the nurse and she was going to explain to Shannon what would happen. The play specialist reassured Shannon that she would stay and help her with her activities throughout. Shannon was given time to get her activities under way.

The nurse told Shannon that she needed to get things started with her left arm. She asked Shannon where she would like her mum to sit and where the play specialist should sit to be able to help her continue her activities.

Shannon asked what was going to happen and the nurse explained that she needed to put a needle into her arm and wrap it up with a bandage. Her mum would help out by cuddling Shannon and holding her arm for her. Shannon showed signs of feeling worried and became upset and tearful – an acceptable and normal response. The play specialist gave Shannon some encouragement, 'You can do it, this is easy for an expert like you,' and distracted her with an activity, 'Let's just play this game on the iPad.' The nurse was able to set up the infusion and Shannon's relief and pleasure in being able to co-operate was enormous.

Managing Pain

Sometimes fear and anxieties associated with hospital are as a result of pain occurring at the hospital due to procedures connected with the treatment or the medical condition itself. Helping your child manage pain is difficult. It is one of those things that can be successful for a while but then something changes and there is a flare-up and the child finds it difficult again. When any of us experiences pain, we perceive it as a threat. This makes it difficult to ignore, and our natural response is either to escape it or to protect ourselves from it. Therefore, it isn't surprising that children will do anything they can to avoid pain and often turn to you to prevent it from occurring. They are only doing what is natural. For you as parents, though, this can be incredibly distressing, especially if there is nothing you can do to avoid the pain, because you know the procedure is necessary for your child's treatment.

Pain and painful procedures can be a regular occurrence for children with physical health conditions. If the main symptom of your child's condition is pain, then this should be managed by a pain specialist and a multidisciplinary team. The focus of this section is in guiding parents who have to help their child occasionally co-operate with a procedure that causes some momentary pain and discomfort: for example, dressing changes.

Case Study – Jonah (10 years old)

Jonah has severe eczema. He needs to have daily creams and occasionally needs a clinic visit to have more creams and dressings. Jonah finds these clinic visits anxiety-provoking and painful. Jonah's dad, David, has asked for some help in managing Jonah when he needs the dressings applied.

This is a difficult situation for Jonah's dad who realises he shouldn't stop the dressings from being changed because this is a necessary part of Jonah's treatment. It is important for you as a parent to believe that you are doing the right thing by looking after your child's health, even if the treatment does result in your child feeling some pain.

It used to be thought that pain was purely a physical phenomenon, which meant that doctors would examine the symptoms reported to be painful, identify a cause and prescribe medication with the expectation that this would stop the pain. However, this doesn't take account of the variation we all have in how we experience pain. In some situations, the experience of pain is reduced; for example, if your child is engrossed in an activity they may tolerate pain more easily than if they are focusing on the pain. Similarly, we are more likely to notice pain if we are worried about it; for example, if we are concerned it is a symptom of something getting worse. There are also differences in how families respond and cope with pain and your views will affect how your children respond to their own symptoms. You may also notice differences between children; maybe you have one child who is very sensitive to pain and another who never complains.

This is due to the complex nature of pain that is a combination of physical messages from nerve endings and an interpretation of these messages made in the brain. We now know that pain is influenced by psychological as well as physical factors, and this means managing pain can make use of both physical and psychological approaches.

There are some ways in which pain can be managed that involve changing the way it is thought about. This does not mean that the pain isn't there or your child is making it up. We now understand that once the nerves send messages to the brain, the brain has the capacity to interpret the pain and this will affect how much it is perceived to hurt. This process is more complicated in children because they don't have enough experience to be able to make sense of this sensation of pain – they need your help to know how to think about pain.

Helping Your Child to Manage Acute Predicted/Repeated Pain

Case Study (cont'd) – Jonah (10 years old)

Jonah and his dad met the psychologist at a time when Jonah did not need any painful procedures done. Jonah was asked to look at a rating chart like this one:

Wong-Baker FACES® Pain Rating Scale

0	2	4	6	8	10
No Hurt	Hurts Little Bit	Hurts Little More	Hurts Even More	Hurts Whole Lot	Hurts Worst

©1983 Wong-Baker FACES Foundation. www.WongBakerFACES.org
Used with permission. Originally published in *Whaley & Wong's Nursing Care of Infants and Children.* ©Elsevier Inc.

Jonah was asked to point to the face that showed how much pain he was in right at that moment. Jonah picked 2. He said he didn't have a lot of pain, but he was a bit worried because he didn't know what was going to happen. This was a very useful example to start with, as it demonstrates that worry and anxiety can also affect the rating of pain as well as painful things happening.

Jonah and his dad made a list together of all the things that are painful for Jonah associated with his hospital visits and they then used the 0-10 rating scale to indicate the level of pain in each situation and put this into a table:

What is happening	Rating Scale
Routine clinic assessment with no treatment done	2
Dressings changed	6
Nurse putting creams on	6
Dad putting creams on	4

Jonah then explained why it was less painful when dad put cream on compared to the nurses. He said dad took longer, allowed him to watch TV and gave him breaks.

The psychologist told Jonah he already seemed like an expert in psychology strategies and explained to him what he was doing and why it helped:

- *Watching TV was making use of distraction, taking his mind off the procedure and focusing on the TV instead*

- *Taking breaks was making use of his rating scale and pacing himself; when he felt the pain moving to the next highest level, he was taking a breather*

- *Jonah and his dad were asked to think of other things they could do to make the pain easier to manage, and they came up with:*

  - *Getting a treat (Jonah's idea) or having something to look forward to (Dad's idea)*

  - *Not focusing on and talking about the procedure*

  - *Going slowly*

  - *Being OK to say it hurts*

  - *Stopping for a breather when Jonah is getting worked up*

  - *Jonah choosing where he sits and what he watches*

Jonah was able to feel included in recognising that he feels pain, feeling believed and knowing it was OK to say he was in pain. He found his rating scale very helpful because he could point to it and show people if it was changing. Jonah also felt like he was making progress because he knew he was already saying yes to having his painful treatments done, rather than everyone talking about this as a problem which was difficult to manage.

Parents Are Part of Pain Management

Though it may be very difficult for you to watch your child in distress, it is important that you are part of the strategy to help manage pain. With children, it is about thinking differently about the pain, and parents can be essential in finding out what their children are thinking. You can help support your child by engaging with coping strategies and focusing on distraction activities and managing pain in everyday situations. Often parents become so concerned about the reports of pain from their child that they continually seek more and more investigations. However, sometimes the best thing you can do as a parent is to help your child with coping strategies. You as parents can:

- Tolerate distress and discomfort in your child without trying to fix it – acknowledge the pain and give comfort

- Be present with your child as a source of comfort

- Learn to respond to and give attention to desirable behaviour, such as coping and engaging in activity rather than behaviour associated with pain or expressions of pain

Swallowing Tablets

We have included this subject in the anxiety and phobia chapter because, although many children do not have any difficulty swallowing tablets, we have found that if difficulties do arise they are often connected with worries and anxieties rather than a problem with technique. The suggested approach can be done with any child, not just those with anxieties about swallowing; it is a practical, calm method of introducing tablet-taking.

Paediatricians generally prefer children to take medications in tablet rather than liquid form (in suspension). This is because the dosage, digestion and absorption of the drug are better in tablet form. For children taking long-term daily medication, it is worth teaching them to swallow tablets from an early age. Children can learn to swallow tablets from about the age of three, and it is best to teach the practice before the age of six years. After this age, they tend to think too much about it, which is where the anxiety comes in. So you are less likely to have difficulties the earlier you start.

If your child is older and it is hard to get them over the initial hurdle of swallowing, there is an approach known as 'pill school' which involves starting with a very small amount of food, and gradually working up in size so that pill-sized amounts can be swallowed. This is a way of desensitising them to the fear of swallowing, which can help them get over their beliefs that they are unable to swallow. If there are problems with this approach in an older child, then you should access support from your medical team such as a nurse specialist or a psychologist.

Children with anxiety or refusal to swallow tablets often believe or fear that the tablet will get stuck in their throat or they will choke. Like the other phobias and worries described above (e.g., needles and blood tests), it often results in anticipatory anxiety, not usually from an actual experience of choking, but from anticipating that this will happen. Very commonly, when a child has difficulties swallowing tablets, one of the parents also reports that they have difficulties with tablets, too, and tend to avoid taking them whenever possible.

So the first thing to do is to check your own thoughts, actions and comments regarding tablet-swallowing. Are you signalling to your child that you are concerned? Think about what you have said; maybe without thinking, you have commented, 'Look at the size . . . he will never be able to swallow that,' or had a look of concern on your face. Children are very good observers and young children take their cues from you. If you are signalling 'worry' then your child will begin to feel an instinctive anticipatory anxiety response and will be apprehensive about it. If you signal 'competence' (i.e., that it is something that can be done), then they will be more likely to give it a go.

The Nine-step Plan

Generally, this is introduced around about three years of age and, as mentioned above, it is best to achieve this before the age of about six years if possible. The idea is to start at a level your child can already achieve and then build on success. Assuming your child has no physiological reason why they can't swallow and they can already swallow food with no difficulty, then they can learn to swallow tablets. The nine steps below will help your child to learn this new skill.

Step 1 – At a usual mealtime, suggest that you and your child (other children can join in) play a game of 'Abracadabra' to see if they can make their food disappear. You need to make sure that you and your child/children have their favourite drink to hand.

Step 2 – Tell everyone to get a really small bit of their food – e.g., one grain of rice, or one Rice Krispie (it is best to choose a food that is already quite soft). You then say that everyone has to get their drink ready, put their one bit of food in their mouth, and then take three sips of a drink. They then open their mouths and say, 'Abracadabra . . . it has disappeared!'

Step 3 – Look around to check the food has gone and praise everyone.

Step 4 – See if your child can do this with a larger amount of food.

Step 5 – Repeat this at any mealtime but don't make it a big deal.

Step 6 – Discuss with your paediatrician that you would like to introduce your child's medication in tablet form, so discuss the dosage and ask for a prescription.

Step 7 – Tell your child that you know that if they can easily make their food disappear then they would easily be able to make a tablet disappear. Show them the tablet and ask if they want to have a go. With younger children build on their desire for achievement; most children can be encouraged by saying things like, 'You would be such a grown-up girl if you can do this . . . I think you can do it.' Older children who show anxiety will need a different approach; you will have to show them that you know they can already do it because they have swallowed larger sizes of food playing the Abracadabra game.

Step 8 – Get their favourite drink ready and repeat the Abracadabra game using the tablet. Obviously, only your child joins in! If they manage it, then give lots of praise, tell family members to increase positive attention and possibly give another small treat.

Step 9 – Tell your child that from now on they can do grown-up tablet-taking. Make it normal practice. If your child has a blip and refuses, do not force the issue: just go back to occasionally playing the Abracadabra game until they build up their confidence again.

Many children learn this very quickly and often surprise their parents. Once tablets can be swallowed, there is rarely any turning back; blips are often quickly overcome because children learn that tablets are much more convenient and quicker than liquid suspension and, more often than not, there is no taste from tablets.

Hospital Phobia in Parents

Sometimes parents find that their child needs to attend hospital on a regular basis and they have to face their own fear of hospitals. In some cases, just the knowledge that their child must go to hospital is enough for the fear to be overcome, but some parents need further support in their own right. The bottom line here is that if you have a hospital phobia and your child needs to go you *will* have to face your fear and get help to manage it. No one can support your child as well as you can, so you need to be able to be there for your child.

Case Study – Stevie (6 years old)

Sean is the father of Stevie, aged six, who has juvenile arthritis. He needs to be seen in clinic regularly and requires occasional admissions for a few nights. Sean and Stevie have a very good relationship, but Sean cannot attend any of the hospital appointments with his son as he has a severe hospital phobia. Stevie gets distressed when he has to be admitted and is often in a lot of pain requiring unpleasant procedures. Sean is aware that he has to face his hospital phobia. This is the step-by-step approach taken with Sean.

Step 1 – Sean was helped to make a plan jointly with the psychologist at Stevie's hospital, starting with his eventual goal of being with Stevie in hospital and working backwards in small steps to the point he is at now, his starting point. We called this the 'hierarchy'. (For young children, other words can be used such as 'goal list' or 'target list'.)

Step 2 – Sean was taught some relaxation techniques to manage anxiety when he felt overwhelmed (see the Resources section at the end of the book for some websites useful for psychological wellbeing).

Step 3 – Sean went through each step on his hierarchy and identified negative thoughts that made it more difficult for him to achieve the steps.

Step 4 – Sean was taught how to challenge each of the negative thoughts, by using an alternative, less anxious thought; we called these his 'safety nets'.

Step 5 – Sean was asked to think of a reward for achieving each of the steps towards his goal.

<u>*Sean's hierarchy*</u>

Starting point – *Driving wife and Stevie to hospital but not going in.*

Negative thought – *I should already be able to do this . . . I feel embarrassed that I can't do it.*

Safety net – *I am already on my way to achieving my target because I have started on this plan and I will be able to drive to the hospital. I don't need to feel embarrassed.*

Reward – *Pleased with myself that I already have the first step under control.*

Building skills – *Going to the hospital on my own but not for any appointments with Stevie.*

Negative thought – *I will just walk by and not be able to go in.*

Safety net – *It is a building that my son is used to, he knows the nurses and doctors, he feels comfortable here, so I can do this.*

Reward – *Tell Stevie that I did it; I've been into his hospital.*

Getting used to it – Visiting the ward during inpatient admission for Stevie.

Negative thought – I won't be able to walk into the hospital.

Safety net – Take calm deep breaths. I am only staying for a short time, I am just going to see if Stevie is OK then go home.

Reward – Proud of self, reassured that I can do this, wife and Stevie pleased.

Making progress – Going to Stevie's outpatient appointment with my wife.

Negative thought – I won't be able to go in and will leave it to my wife.

Safety net – I am with my wife, it isn't like a hospital, it is a building and my wife knows what to expect.

Reward – All out for lunch afterwards.

Nearly there – Take Stevie to his outpatient appointment alone.

Negative thought – I will panic and will have to go home and Stevie will miss his appointment.

Safety net – *Calm deep breaths, Stevie knows what is going on, I have already done this, I know what to expect, nothing bad happens.*

Reward – *Toy shop on the way home for Stevie.*

Target – *Go to hospital and stay overnight with Stevie.*

Negative thought – *I will panic and have to leave which will upset Stevie.*

Safety net – *If I sense panic, I do my calm deep breaths, I tell myself, 'You can stay, this is just a building, I am just staying in my son's bedroom.'*

Reward – *Proud of myself, trip to cinema with family.*

Sean worked though his steps with the help of his family and he was able to repeat any step as often as he liked before he felt he was ready to move to the next. After a few months, Sean achieved his target goal.

Most hospitals will have hospital play specialists or clinical psychologists who are experts in techniques to help control anxiety associated with procedures and tests. You should ask your doctor or nurse about getting help from a clinical psychologist or play specialist if you think you and your child can benefit from some of the strategies mentioned in this chapter.

Key Points

- Anxiety and fear are normal reactions to frightening or painful procedures.

- It is important for you as parents to feel confident when helping your child with procedures – you have the difficult task of trying to make sure your child gets the right treatment but also having to manage your child's distress.

- Be assertive about asking for time to plan the procedure if you feel you or your child needs this – it is better to spend time on this than to cancel a procedure.

- There are a variety of techniques to use – these are best planned in advance to choose the right approach for each individual child.

- Keep anticipatory anxiety to a minimum by planning before the procedure and giving the child some limited choices when this is possible.

- Hospital play specialists can help with preparation for procedures and distraction during procedures.

- Clinical psychologists can help when the problem interferes with treatment and if the child has more generalised anxiety; for example, worries about a lot of things, or if the anxiety is so severe that you as parents would like further help.

5

Managing Your Child's Behaviour around Medical Procedures

In this chapter, we will look at some of the behavioural difficulties that are common in children and ways of managing these. The techniques that are used to manage the behaviour of healthy children can work for children with physical health conditions, with some adaptations. However, it may be harder for you as a parent to put these into practice for several reasons. For example, your child might be unwell, and you need them to co-operate with treatment so the usual parenting tactics such as removing something they like – such as watching TV or playing on a tablet – might seem too harsh and unreasonable. You might feel that with everything they have been through and continue to go through to stay well, you just want them to have a positive time and can't bring yourself to limit your child. So, we will look at some of the reasons for this and make some suggestions as to how you can overcome the issue.

Being 'Normal' Children

All children will show some behaviour that challenges their parents or carers at times. It is natural for children to want their own way, to want nice things to happen and to continue to happen, and all children want to avoid doing things that they consider to be unpleasant or inconvenient. Babies are hard-wired from birth to get their carers to respond to their needs. They are known to change their cries and noises to indicate different needs and very quickly babies will cry not just because they are hungry, not just because they need their nappy changing, but simply because they want attention.

So, in essence, from the word 'go' babies shape their parents' behaviour and this is how a parent and infant learn to communicate with each other.

Your job as a parent includes providing nurture, nourishment and safety, and promoting your child's development and learning. This requires getting your baby or child to do certain things and not others. For example, during weaning, your baby has to learn to accept a whole range of food types, not just sweet foods. Parents encourage their baby to move and crawl but prevent them from crawling into dangerous places. Many parents will have learned that, from the start, their infant is extremely good at letting them know their personal preferences. The tiny infant will be adept at spitting out non-preferred tastes, at repeatedly crawling towards the stairs despite being stopped each time, and so on. So, be reassured: conflict, opposition and challenge are a normal part of parenting. Challenging, difficult behaviour occurs throughout childhood and adolescence, as you can see from each of the examples below which illustrate normal behaviour across different age groups.

Case Study – Bailey (5 months old)

Bailey is the second child in the family. She has an older brother Tyler, aged two, who is an active toddler, but mum describes him as having been an easy baby. In contrast, Bailey has always seemed more difficult; she takes a long time to feed, has been colicky, doesn't sleep for long periods and only settles when she is held. Bailey only seems content when mum is holding her, and she cries when mum tries to put her down. She has started to cry if anyone else holds her and seems to only want mum. Her cries get very loud if mum doesn't pick her up immediately.

Bailey's mum feels tired, exhausted and at a loss as to how to manage this.

Case Study – Zahir (4 years old)

Zahir has an older sister, Zara, who is seven years old. Mum says Zahir has tantrums whenever he can't have his own way. She says he seems to know exactly when to have them, so she has to give in. For example, Zahir will scream and cry when mum says he has to do something, so she is often late collecting her daughter from school because Zahir refuses to leave the house or the park or put on his coat.

Zahir's mum feels that every day brings conflict and tantrums. She doesn't want to give in but sometimes feels she has no option.

Case Study – Miriam (8 years old)

Miriam has two older sisters aged nine and eleven and a younger sister aged four. Miriam is described by her stepfather as strong-willed. He says she is very intelligent and can be very loving towards her younger sister but once she has made her mind up about something, no amount of reasoning can change it.

Miriam's stepfather says he thinks she sometimes creates arguments just for the sake of it. For example, insisting she sits in the front seat of the car can create an argument that goes on for hours. She has recently decided that she won't eat anything green.

Miriam's stepfather says she is exhausting, and he has tried everything he can think of to try to avoid conflict and arguments.

Case Study – Andrew (15 years old)

Andrew is the oldest of three children; he has a brother aged twelve and a sister aged ten. Andrew's parents say they don't know him any more as he never communicates with them. Andrew comes home from school and goes straight to his bedroom. He takes his food to his room, hardly speaks to his parents and is rude to his brother and sister. If they ask him to join the family or bring down his used plates, he ignores them or yells. Despite this, Andrew is doing well in school and his teachers say he is well behaved and sociable.

Andrew's parents have tried threats to remove his laptop and phone. They have tried offering treats and rewards if he carries out a chore, but nothing works to make a long-term change.

Bailey, Zahir, Miriam and Andrew are all showing behaviours typical of their ages and stages of development. None of them have problems – they are just doing what comes naturally to maintain the things in life that give them pleasure. For Bailey, this means keeping her mum close to her. For Zahir, this means doing what he wants to do, rather than what his mother wants him to do. For Miriam, this means wanting to be in control and getting her own way, so she is bossy and argumentative. For Andrew, this means being a teenager and doing things that most of his friends will value, such as gaming or social media contacts.

When Your Child is Unwell

Some of you reading these examples may feel that you wish you had such simple parenting issues. For you, your child's health condition has meant your child has always had other more important things to cope with. Common difficulties, such as the examples above, are easier to manage if you have a healthy child. At times, all parents have to demonstrate 'tough love' and do something that their child will not like but which will benefit them in the longer term. While applying 'tough love', parenting can be difficult for any parent; when your child has been born with a serious medical condition, has become unwell or has long-term physical and/or developmental needs requiring constant attention and daily treatment, your priorities as a parent may well be focused on managing their health needs, and managing their behaviour may seem less important.

There are three factors commonly reported by parents that affect their parenting style: the impact of the diagnosis; the impact on their confidence as a parent; and, finally, being able to be firm with a child who already has additional difficulties due to their health condition.

First, impact of diagnosis – as discussed in Chapter 2, the time of diagnosis can be overwhelming emotionally and even traumatic, and many parents report that from this moment there is a shift in how they see their relationship with their child. In a way, many parents feel the need to become 'super parents' in order to manage the additional responsibility of their child's illness, as well as managing the normal or typical difficulties any healthy child might experience.

Second, lack or loss of confidence as a parent – many parents report a loss of confidence or difficulty in establishing a comfortable role as a parent in authority. These comments are so frequently reported as to be completely normal in themselves. In fact, many health professionals very often marvel at the amount of daily tasks achieved by parents of children requiring so much medical treatment and clinic appointments, as well as juggling family life and work – but parents often have no idea they are held in such high esteem; more often than not, they think the opposite.

Third, being firm feels like punishment – it is much harder to set limits and stick to them when you hate to see your child unhappy, especially when you feel they have enough hardship in their life already. However, sometimes being a loving parent also includes 'tough love' – in the short term the child might not be happy with the limits or rules you set, but in the long term they will benefit from the security of boundaries.

Being a 'Good Enough' Parent

Every few years a new trend or fashionable childcare manual appears – there are thousands of them. However, there are some basic parenting principles that will always work no matter what the fashion or challenges. There is also one very important thing to remember: there is no 'perfect' way to be a parent. It is not always easy, so set your expectations at an achievable level and aim to be a 'good enough' parent rather than a 'perfect' parent.

Many parenting experts make a similar statement at the start of their advice: being a good enough parent requires one basic feature – love for your child. What all the comments from parents above describe is their love for their child. A very strong need to protect your child because of their fragility due to their medical condition can lead to particularly intense feelings of protectiveness.

Top Ten Parenting Techniques

The following guide shows the Top Ten parenting techniques that work if done correctly and consistently. The section after that shows how the techniques can be applied in real-life examples for a range of behavioural difficulties and age ranges of children.

Top Ten Parenting Techniques

1 – Avoid unnecessary confrontations

Save it for when it matters – if they want to wear wellies when it's hot, why not? You don't need to control everything, so better to save the effort for the important things you do need to control.

Age range: Especially good for pre-school age.

2 – Distract and divert attention

Really works with young children; when you sense a battle building, quickly point out something interesting and head off any approaching conflict.

Age range: Especially good for pre-school age.

---

3 – State clear expectations

Don't ask a question if you want compliance. We very often ask a question when we aren't really giving an option. For example, we might say, 'Would you like to do your treatment now?' What you actually mean is: 'It is time to do your treatment now.' Make your intention clear and, whenever possible, in a positive way. For example: 'I am going to put your favourite programme on the TV and we will do your treatment while we watch it . . .' or 'You can watch TV now while you do your nebuliser.'

Age range: Good technique for all ages.

4 – Ignore tantrums whenever you can

They are intended to get your attention. If you give it, they will get louder; let them fizzle out by ignoring them whenever you can.

Age range: Especially for early childhood, though watch out for teenage tantrums – e.g., door slamming and shouting. They are often better ignored than confronted as the confrontation can make them worse.

5 – Cut down on commands

Notice how often you tell your child what to do compared to how much time is spent in to-and-fro conversation. Use 'descriptive commenting' where you just describe or comment on what it is they are doing and use positive comments when possible:

'You are setting up the farm with all those animals really well . . .'

'Thanks for your help bringing down your laundry . . . it's so good when I don't have to nag you.'

Age range: All ages benefit from this technique.

6 – Decrease the number of times you say 'no'

Many parents find themselves saying 'no' more often than they tell their child what would be better to do instead. Rather than saying, 'No, you can't play on the iPad now . . .' try saying, 'When you've done your reading, then you can have some time on the iPad.'

Age range: All ages benefit from this technique.

7 – Give attention for what you want to see, not what you don't

Parents often spend more time with their child when they are doing something they shouldn't be doing, rather than when they are doing something well. Children thrive on attention – if they are getting attention mostly when they are doing something they shouldn't, they will still enjoy this type of attention, too. Teenagers are also thirsty for attention and will often do something reckless or risky to get a response from you.

Age range: All ages benefit from this technique.

8 – Don't criticise

No one likes it. If you want to encourage your child to do something well, praise any attempt they make, even if it is far from perfect.

Age range: Older children and teenagers benefit from this technique. Teenagers can be particularly sensitive to criticism.

9 – Set limits and boundaries

Boundaries give children a sense of security and that you are looking out for them, and young children need parental guidance and to be told when enough is enough. A 'boundary' is letting your child know what is acceptable and what is not and sticking to your rule. If you say only one biscuit before dinner, then keep to your rule. It is the same for older children; if you say electronic equipment has to be switched off at 10 p.m., then make sure you stick to your rule.

Age range: All ages benefit from this technique.

10 – Be consistent

If you set a limit or consequence, stick to it. Children quickly realise when they can argue their way out of a consequence. Don't threaten them with something you can never follow through on.

Age range: All ages benefit from this technique.

How to Apply the Techniques in Real Life

The following case examples illustrate the use of the techniques given above. When you are in the middle of managing a difficult situation, it is not always easy to be able to identify for yourself exactly what it is that you are doing, or your child is doing, that is contributing to the difficulty. If you read through these examples, this may help you to think about some of the possibilities as identified by other parents. Using the checklist of ten techniques should also help you to identify if one of these could be relevant to what is happening.

There is a four-step approach to considering how to change the way you manage your child's behavioural difficulties:

Step 1 – Take a step back and think about what is going on in this situation. 'What am I doing? Why isn't it working?'

Step 2 – Use the table to identify the parenting techniques that you are currently using and review how well they are working.

Step 3 – Build on your successes and parenting skills. 'When am I successful at getting my children to do what I say?'

Step 4 – Make a plan of action; what to ignore, what to say, what technique to use.

It may help to talk it through with someone you trust – your partner or a good friend or relative – since they can help you 'step back' and reflect on what is happening. It is not always easy to do this on your own. It is also helpful to have them on board, so they are using the same consistent techniques.

Common Problem 1 – My Child Won't Co-operate with His Medical Treatment

Case Study – James (9 years old)

James has cystic fibrosis (CF). This is a life-long genetic condition for which there is currently no cure, but improved treatments mean people with CF can now expect good quality and quantity of life. However, in order to achieve that there is a daily treatment regime of tablets and chest physiotherapy as well as regular clinic visits to monitor lung health and any infections. James needs to take daily tablets (vitamins and antibiotics); a pancreatic enzyme supplement when eating food containing fat; do chest physiotherapy exercises twice a day; and nebulisers containing antibiotics and drugs to thin secretions in the lungs several times a day.

James lives with his mother and an older brother who doesn't have CF. James has got fed up of all the things he has to do every day because he has CF. James feels well, like a 'normal' boy, so he joins in all the same things as his friends at school and he can't see the point of having to do all this treatment. James's mum is at the end of her tether. She knows how important the daily treatments are for keeping James well. James used to do everything very well but now he runs away and won't do it. James's mum has tried what she calls blackmail: 'If you do it, then I will buy you some something as a treat.' She has tried what she calls threats: 'If you don't do it, I will take your iPad away.' Nothing seems to make a difference.

James's mum's approach

James's mum followed the four steps to help her understand what was and was not working:

Step 1 – Take a step back

What is going on? What am I doing? Why isn't it working?

James's mum could see that she has become so concerned about his condition that when she thinks about James her focus is totally on his CF and treatment. She has placed it uppermost in her mind and so, as soon as James gets in from school, she is 'prepared for battle', with her sole concern being him getting his medical treatment. From James's perspective, CF was not the most important thing in his life. He was much more interested in playing with friends at school and games on his iPad.

Step 2 – Review current parenting techniques (from Top Ten techniques above)

James's mum saw she was making some errors:

Technique number 3 – 'State clear expectations': James's mum realised that she was not being clear and had resorted to nagging. She would say, 'James – physio!' ... 'James – nebuliser!' but wasn't clear about how, what and when.

Technique number 5 – 'Cut down on commands': James's mum was issuing a lot of commands and getting increasingly irate as James refused to co-operate.

Technique number 7 – 'Give attention to what you want to see, not what you don't want': James's mum considered this to be where she was mostly going wrong. She predicted from the outset that James would be difficult and so almost immediately she would say something like, 'No arguments tonight, treatment is getting done.' James would disappear, and she would shout intermittently, 'Come on, treatment now.' She gave him lots of attention for not doing his treatment.

Technique number 8 – 'Don't criticise': James's mum recognised that she was being very critical of James for not doing his treatment and that a lot of the comments she made to him were focused on CF and her disappointment in him that he was not co-operating.

Step 3 – Build on your successes and parenting skills:
'When am I successful at getting my children to do what I say?'

James's mum identified that she was able to get both her boys to follow certain household rules in that they were polite and helped with some chores and James would get dressed and ready for bed easily. Thinking about one of these tasks – e.g., cleaning teeth – James's mum could see that she was not making any parenting errors and was following the strategies by:

Technique number 3 – 'State clear expectations': Being clear about her expectation about cleaning teeth before bed and ensuring that James knew how to do it.

Technique number 7 – 'Give attention for what you want to see, not what you don't want': Giving attention for what she wanted so that James knew his mum was pleased with him for being ready at bedtime.

Technique number 8 – 'Don't criticise': Though cleaning teeth might seem like a minor achievement, James's mum remembered that she was very good at teaching James and how pleased he was with her satisfaction in his success.

Step 4 – Plan of action

James's mum decided to start with one small part of the treatment routine – one nebuliser – and identified the following strategies to put into practice:

- **Clear expectations** – She worked out how to make clear to James what the new rule was and what she expected of him. She would get the nebuliser ready and sit with him while he did it.

- **Attention for what she wants to see** – She agreed with James what they would do together while he used his nebuliser and that she would stay with him until it was done.

- **Praise** – Giving praise and approval for completing the nebuliser, then the task is completed and James is free to get on with other things of his choosing.

- **Gradual build-up of new treatment tasks** – This is so that James gradually builds up the required tasks, resulting eventually in all his daily treatments being accomplished. This should be through a phased process at a pace that results in them being successfully done and not pushed all at once.

Common Problem 2 – My Child Won't Co-operate in the Clinic

Case Study – Tanya (6 years old)

Tanya was diagnosed with epilepsy a year ago. She has two older half-brothers aged eleven and thirteen. Her oldest brother has a diagnosis of autistic spectrum disorder.

Unfortunately, Tanya continues to have frequent seizures and is having regular reviews with the neurology clinic. At each clinic appointment, Tanya must be weighed and measured to check the correct dosage of any medications that might be prescribed. She needs to have telemetry [measurement of brain activity] which requires her to wear a helmet, and she needs to be seen by the neurologist and sometimes the neuropsychologist to check her learning and development.

As soon as Tanya arrives in clinic, she heads for the toys and then refuses to budge. Mum frequently has to carry her to the room to be weighed and sit on the scales with her. Very often, Tanya's height cannot be accurately measured. Tanya has a tantrum when called to the telemetry room and the technicians cannot conduct the procedure. The neurologist has to make treatment recommendations based on mum's report rather than an accurate measurement. Mum is concerned that the medical team think she isn't a good mother and that Tanya will get worse and require a hospital admission.

Tanya's mum's approach

Step 1 – Take a step back

What is going on? What am I doing? Why isn't it working?

Tanya's mum recognised that she had been overwhelmed by the diagnosis and worried that she would not be able to cope as she already found managing her eldest son with autistic spectrum disorder to be very difficult. Tanya's mum acknowledged that she had not been very good at being firm with Tanya and was already losing confidence in her abilities as a mother and believed that the medical team were critical of her.

Step 2 – Review current parenting techniques

Tanya's mum thought that the main area where she was going wrong was with technique number 9 – not setting sufficient limits or boundaries. When arriving in the clinic, Tanya's mum felt helpless and just crossed her fingers that Tanya would behave. She recognised that Tanya could be feeling scared and chaotic, exactly the way she was feeling.

Step 3 – Build on your successes and parenting skills:
'When am I successful at getting my children to do what I say?'

Tanya's mum felt that there were lots of times when she enjoyed being with Tanya and described Tanya as being very creative. She could see that she was good at giving attention for what she wanted to see when Tanya was making pictures and models. She was good at giving praise, accepting Tanya's decisions, valuing what she created, and she didn't interfere or criticise when Tanya made things.

Step 4 – Plan of action

Tanya's mum decided that her first action was to anticipate that Tanya was worried about going to the clinic and having all the procedures and so she planned to go to the appointment armed with a bag full of creative activities to distract Tanya.

Therefore, Tanya's mum was clear they were going to the weighing room and she discussed in advance what activity would happen in there; mum was ready to be full of praise for Tanya showing any small sign of co-operation and ready to ignore any tantrum by focusing her attention on the clinic staff and discussing the creative activity they had brought with them with the idea that this would engage Tanya in her art.

Tanya's mum also planned to be more confident herself, to inform the neurology team that she was trying to support Tanya's worries, and her own, and to discuss with the medical team whether it would be possible to reduce the number of tests and assessments attempted in clinic in order to increase the chance of being able to complete them successfully.

Common Problem 3 – My Child Gets Upset and Sad When She Has to Go into Hospital

Case Study – Ayesha (10 years old)

Ayesha has kidney disease and needs regular admissions for kidney dialysis. This has to be done in hospital for safety reasons. Ayesha needs to be attached to the dialysis machine and stay at the bedside for several hours. Ayesha is an only child; she is intelligent, and her parents report that she is always well behaved and quite an easy child.

However, whenever her admission approaches she cries and cries and begs her parents not to take her. Both parents have tried reasoning with her, explaining why they must take her, but Ayesha says she hates it, hates being ill and wishes she was someone else. Both parents are heartbroken when they arrive. Ayesha is always silent during her admission; she reads her books by her bedside.

Ayesha's parents' approach

Step 1 – Take a step back

What is going on? What am I doing? Why isn't it working?

Ayesha's parents acknowledged she was a very precious child as she was the only one they had managed to conceive, although they wanted more. Mum reported that she always felt slightly ostracised from some family members for only having one child, so Ayesha's diagnosis had hit them hard and they were constantly fearful they would lose her. It was difficult for Ayesha's parents to ask for emotional help from health professionals because, within their own culture, it was not considered acceptable to discuss concerns outside the family. Mum could see that their tendency to be private was also mirrored by Ayesha.

Step 2 – Review current parenting techniques

Ayesha's parents identified that they were ending up struggling with technique number 7 – they were actually giving attention for what they *didn't* want to see. Although Ayesha's parents were giving appropriate attention to her worries, they were inadvertently reinforcing her repeated patterns of behaviour. The strategies they had tried were not successful, but they were at a loss what else to do. There was a feeling of acceptance of the status quo and that nothing could change.

Step 3 – Build on your successes and parenting skills:
'When am I successful at getting my children to do what I say?'

Technique number 1 – 'Avoid unnecessary confrontations': Ayesha's parents were very good at positive parenting, Ayesha was a polite and well-behaved girl, and they avoided unnecessary confrontation.

Technique number 7 – 'Give attention for what you want to see, not what you don't': Ayesha's parents were excellent at demonstrating how proud they were of everything Ayesha did.

Step 4 – Plan of action

They planned to use techniques number 4 and 2 – ignoring Ayesha's tantrums, and distracting her wherever possible. Although Ayesha had good reason to become upset prior to her admission, the pattern of behaviour needed to be broken. The family had to break the habit of reinforcing Ayesha's crying and divert it instead.

They also planned to use technique number 9 – setting clear boundaries. Ayesha's parents had to be firm; there was no choice about the admission and it was out of their control. As good, responsible and loving parents they had to take care of her health and wellbeing, and that required her medical treatment. They could not therefore give in to her request to not take her to hospital. They could, though, help her think of things she could do while she was in hospital.

Common Problem 4 – My Child Hates Having Procedures Done

Case Study – Daniel (4 years old)

Daniel has a diagnosis of coeliac disease. This means he cannot digest certain food types and needs a restricted diet as well as daily medication. Daniel needs to go to hospital clinics regularly to have a range of tests done to monitor the progress of the disease and how well the diet and medication are doing at keeping the disease under control. These tests vary each time he attends depending on his symptoms and on the recommended timings of different tests.

Sometimes Daniel needs to have blood taken, scans of his stomach and bowel, or more invasive tests which require an anaesthetic and a look though a camera. Daniel is too young to understand why he needs to have visits to hospital and then painful or uncomfortable procedures done to him.

Daniel has a baby brother and lives with both his parents. Daniel's mother reports that he 'hits refusal mode' as soon as they arrive at the hospital. Both parents have to bring him to the clinic in order to support each other and help manage what they predict will be difficult behaviour in Daniel. Mum feels guilty at having to leave his brother behind, as well as knowing she is going to have to force Daniel to have horrible things done. His parents often have to hold Daniel tightly to make sure procedures can be done without accidental injury. She worries about the long-term emotional damage that might be done by going through this regularly.

Daniel's parents' approach

Step 1 – Take a step back

What is going on? What am I doing? Why isn't it working?

Daniel's parents recognised that they had the view that he had suffered enough. They felt that he had been through so much and that they had become angry at his medical diagnosis and frustrated with the medical team who seemed to continually assess him. They recognised that they had also somewhat 'hit refusal mode'. From Daniel's perspective, they acknowledged that he was always having horrid things done to him and they felt powerless to prevent them. Rather than think of ways to help him manage the procedures, they wanted to stop them from occurring.

Step 2 – Review current parenting techniques

Daniel's parents could see that they were less successful with technique number 3 – not being able to set clear expectations of what they would do and what he would do on arrival in clinic, in part because they were never completely sure what would be required, but also because they predicted he would refuse to have the tests or procedures.

Technique number 7 – 'Giving attention for what you want to see . . .': Mum recognised that she spent a lot of time trying to cajole him, so – without meaning to – was giving him lots of attention for refusing to co-operate.

Technique number 10 – 'Be consistent': Mum was able to see that she didn't stick to the boundaries for much of Daniel's behaviour and neither did his father; they both wanted to be good cop and hoped someone else would step in and be bad cop.

Step 3 – Build on your successes and parenting skills: 'When am I successful at getting my children to do what I say?'

Mum and dad said they were both good at praising and managing Daniel's diet. It had been difficult finding ways to distract him from forbidden foods, but they had been creative, and Daniel was now very accepting and starting to know himself what he couldn't eat.

Step 4 – Plan of action

Daniel's parents felt they needed to gain more control over the clinic visits so that they had a clearer expectation of what the visits would involve. So they decided to put into action techniques number 9 and 10 around setting boundaries and being consistent. First, they needed to be clear with Daniel that he was going to have the test; he could choose which parent sat with him and which toy or treat he could have afterwards. Both parents had to agree to and stick to the same rules.

They also implemented techniques number 5, 6 and 8 around fewer commands, reducing saying 'no', and cutting out the criticising. Both parents cut down on commands and just restated the one instruction. They decreased the number of times they told Daniel off or said 'no' or 'don't do that', and gave him attention for following one instruction instead.

They were very aware that they frequently used questions when they didn't mean to. They noted that they said, 'Daniel, shall we go with this lady?' hoping that Daniel would see it was her desire to do the horrid test and not theirs but, in fact, Daniel assumed his parents were giving him a choice and so was angrier when they didn't do as he said when he replied 'No!'

Common Problem 5 – My Child is Really Aggressive and Disobedient at Home after We Have Been to Hospital

Case Study – Morgan (7 years old)

Morgan has a diagnosis of leukaemia. So far, she has been admitted to hospital four times for five to six days each time. She has had treatment that has been painful and unpleasant; she has to stay in her cubicle when having her treatment and has missed a lot of school. Thankfully, she is responding well to treatment and the expectations are that she will make a good recovery and will soon return to her normal life.

> *Morgan has an older sister aged nine and lives with her*
> *mum and stepdad. They report that as soon as Morgan*
> *is home after discharge from hospital she becomes aggres-*
> *sive, often physically aggressive to her sister. Morgan*
> *refuses to do anything she is asked to do if she doesn't*
> *want to do it and the family 'walks on eggshells'. Mum is*
> *worried that she has lost any authority over her daugh-*
> *ter and Morgan has become 'not a nice girl' as a result*
> *of her illness. Mum is also worried about the effect it*
> *has had on her other daughter, who always gives in to*
> *Morgan.*

Morgan's parents' approach

Step 1 – Take a step back

What is going on? What am I doing? Why isn't it working?

Morgan's mum said that the diagnosis had been the beginning of a shift in her relationship with her daughter. The
diagnosis was devastating and traumatic and she had
expected her daughter to die. Information from the hospital team and other parents on social media had been
supportive and Morgan's mother became more optimistic
about the prognosis. However, she recognised that her
initial reaction was one of fear for her daughter and for
herself. Mum and stepdad were also aware that the trauma

and uncertainty around the diagnosis had meant it was almost a taboo subject within the family It was not easily talked about and they didn't really know what Morgan or her sister felt or understood.

Step 2 – Review current parenting techniques

Technique number 9 – 'Set limits and boundaries': In thinking about Morgan's behaviour at home, both mum and stepdad could see that limit-setting was their biggest problem area. They had been very accepting of Morgan's disobedience and were not in a stable frame of mind to be able to do anything about it.

Step 3 – Build on your successes and parenting skills:
'When am I successful at getting my children to do what I say?'

Mum and stepdad knew that things settled down after a few days of leaving hospital and Morgan became manageable. They recognised that their other daughter was always well-behaved which must mean that they had some good parenting skills.

Step 4 – Plan of action

Mum and stepdad decided that they needed to start by talking more openly with the children about leukaemia and to take advice from the healthcare team.

They also recognised that they needed to consider applying techniques number 9 and 10 – setting boundaries and being consistent. They realised that they needed to redress the balance in the home and ensure both girls understood that disobedience and aggression were not acceptable, that it would not now be possible for Morgan to get away with it and unacceptable for her sister to have to put up with it.

Key Points

- Tantrums, opposition and difficult behaviour are a normal part of childhood development.

- There are some fundamental parenting techniques that underpin basic behaviour management.

- Being a good enough parent of a child with a physical health condition can be more challenging due to the:

  * Impact of the diagnosis

  * Confidence levels in being able to cope with the demands of the diagnosis

  * Being able to impose firm boundaries with children who seem to suffer enough

- Typical challenges surround managing treatments, clinic attendance, investigations and tests and admissions.

- Parents can be helped to review their parenting practice and goals by taking a stepped approach:

  * Take a step back

  * Review parenting techniques in relation to the illness challenges

> *   Review current successful parenting practices
>
> *   Plan of action for areas of redressing the balance, bringing about change
>
> - If you find it hard to be able to take a 'step back' from the situation or if you find you can't identify these steps yourself, you may want to get further advice – ask your medical team or your GP for advice about who could help.

6

Feeding Difficulties and Disturbed Eating Attitudes and Behaviours

Feeding difficulties are very common in healthy children as well as in children with a long-term illness, and health visitors are often asked for help with managing feeding. Feeding difficulties tend to fall into two main categories: not eating enough and fussy eating (not eating a sufficiently wide range of foods). The approaches to these two difficulties are broadly the same in terms of how you can understand the problem and make changes. We start with two case examples and then describe the approach to take.

Case Study – Aliya (6 years old)

Aliya is six years old; she lives with both her parents. She is the oldest of four children; she has a brother aged five and two sisters aged four and two. Aliya was born with a heart condition called pulmonary hypertension and she needs regular reviews from a specialist cardiac centre and has daily medication. Although Aliya has no special dietary needs, it is important that she maintains good weight gain as she may need surgery in the future. Mum, Maia, says that Aliya has never had a good appetite and she has always had to offer food more frequently than Aliya would naturally ask for it. Aliya is always the first to finish at mealtimes, as if she would prefer to be doing something else. Maia says that her other children all enjoy eating; she can often use food as a treat or reward for them, but for Aliya that never works.

Dieticians monitoring Aliya's growth have shown mum that although she has always been on the lower end of the expected weight for her age, over the last few months her weight has started to drop off her expected centiles. The medical team discuss with mum that it is important to get more calories into Aliya. Although the dieticians suggest ways of increasing the calories, her mum knows that it will be hard work.

Not Eating Enough

Even in healthy children we know that poor eating is common, but it can get better quite quickly. However, when you have a child like Aliya with a physical illness, and medical professionals who stress the importance of getting calories into her, most parents find their anxiety and worry is sky-high. The risk is that all mealtimes become something to be avoided, scary, horrible and no one wants to be there, let alone eat anything.

Fussy Eaters

Case Study – George (4 years old)

George has a kidney condition called bilateral renal hypoplasia which means that when he was born, both his kidneys were very small. He is monitored and doing well. He is an only child living with both parents. Although George is gaining weight, his parents are worried about his eating as he is very fussy. He will eat fairly large portions but only of a small range of foods he likes, and limited in texture. He will only eat food mum or dad have cooked. He likes a very smooth texture, without lumps and absolutely refuses any change.

George needs calories so his parents are very reluctant to 'rock the boat' by making any changes. They are worried about him starting school as they think he will go the whole day without eating.

George's story is also common in his age group. George's parents might have found that they would have been more confident at making changes to the food they offer him if he didn't have a physical health condition. Like Maia, Aliya's mum, their anxiety is higher because of the importance of a high-calorie intake for their children's continued good health. Both case examples show that the approach to managing feeding difficulties when a child has a physical health condition requires expertise and sensitivity. Quick-fix suggestions are not easily implemented when parents know that their child's health could rapidly deteriorate if weight loss occurs.

Understanding the Problem

The first step for making recommendations for change involves an assessment of all the issues. We have provided an example of a Feeding Behaviour Assessment (opposite), which you might find helpful to fill in to help you identify the key issues for your child.

Though this assessment might seem very detailed, it is helpful to review all these factors to see not only where things are going wrong, but also where things are going right. You might find that this assessment gives you an idea of where the difficulties are occurring and so where to focus your efforts.

Area for Assessment	Definition	Response
Height/weight/growth pattern	Is your child following their predicted rate of growth? (You need to check this with your health visitor or medical team.)	
	What are your and the healthcare team's expectations about what your child should weigh? Are there any differences between what you would like your child to weigh and what the healthcare team think?	
Feeding behaviour	What does your child do when presented with food?	
	Are feeding skills age appropriate? e.g., by four years old most children can feed themselves, cope with most textures and participate in a family meal.	
	Are textures and range of foods age-appropriate? e.g., is your child sticking to just one or two food types? Are they able to eat textures appropriate to their stage of development?	
	Does your child sit still to finish a meal?	
	Is your child hiding food or throwing it on the floor?	
	Is the length of time taken to eat within reasonable limits? Most children eat as much as they are able to in about twenty minutes.	

Area for Assessment	Definition	Response
Medical complications	Are there any medical reasons why eating and digestion may be difficult?	
Feeding history	What has been your child's experience of feeding since birth? Has your child been weaned? Can they manage lumps and chew appropriately? Has your child had any unpleasant experiences associated with food; e.g., vomiting?	
Parental management techniques	How effective are you at ensuring your child sits to eat their food? What are the 'rules' around mealtimes? Do you feel comfortably in control at your child's mealtime? How are you at managing your child's behaviour generally?	
Medical team requirement	What are the prescribed calorie requirements? Do you think these are realistic and achievable? Do you feel pressurised or supported by the team around feeding your child?	

Accuracy of child's calorie intake	Parents often underestimate the calorie intake of their child. How accurate are you being in measuring what your child has eaten? Are you assuming they have not eaten a lot of calories because they haven't finished everything you gave them? Be prepared to make a more accurate assessment of what your child has eaten. Are mealtime observations possible so the medical team/dieticians can see?
Family relationships	Is there support or tension in any of your family relationships regarding feeding or the medical diagnosis?
Demographic variables/lifestyle	Is your family home set up to make mealtimes clear? Do you announce mealtimes? Does everyone join in? Do you stop what you are doing to have a meal or does everyone snack whenever they are hungry? Is there a defined place to eat? Are you able to buy the sort of food that the medical team recommends?

Making Changes

In general, when changing feeding behaviour in young children, there needs to be some consideration of what is happening at different levels. First, the content of the mealtime itself – exactly what food is offered, when and how. Then second, at the child level – exactly how you manage your child at the mealtime, what you do and how you manage the process of the meal itself. So make sure you know in advance what food you are going to give your child and how you are going to manage the whole mealtime. Mealtimes involve not just the child and food, but also the parent and other family members.

You have to take into account instructions from the medical team as well as practicalities like a place to eat and buying the necessary food (which might be expensive). Changing mealtime behaviour can be stressful and difficult. It is important that as parents you get the support you need from the medical team as well as practical and financial help if necessary. You may need to ask the medical team, your health visitor or social work department at your child's hospital.

The following plan is an example of what you may need to do to make changes to mealtimes and manage your child:

1. Mealtime management

Dietetic and medical requirements and goals should be established first. Get some agreement from the medical team about the ideal and minimum acceptable dietary intake. Make sure you are clear about the exact meals to be offered in terms of what type of food, the texture and quantity. For example, with Aliya above, there was agreement that setting a weight target would cause mum more anxiety at mealtimes if Aliya refused or ate very little. The best tactic was to focus instead on Aliya eating and finishing. Mum gave smaller portions and took advice from the dieticians about sources of additional calories that did not cause Aliya to feel too full.

Organisation of mealtimes

There needs to be agreement in your family on who is present and who is in charge. It is very easy for people to offer well-meaning advice, but if there are too many instructions, this can cause confusion for your child and undermine you.

The person who prepares the meal must be in agreement with the recommended food offered. There should be one person in charge and everyone needs to respect that person and support the methods being used. Mealtimes should occur in a consistent place (the usual place for all the family to eat). It is easiest to manage the food given and eaten if it is on a plate at a table, or suitable eating area. However, children often want to eat while watching TV or playing with electronic devices. It is important that you as a parent decide where the meal is going to take place and stick with it. It should be where you feel you have most control over what is going on and the focus can be on eating.

2. Child management

Mealtimes can become very stressful for parents of children with medical conditions who refuse to eat sufficient quantities. When parents become very stressed or anxious, this can result in negative interactions with the child at mealtimes. Consequently, both parent and child come to find mealtimes unpleasant rather than enjoyable. To change this, mealtimes have to be repositioned as times where fun happens. For example, you might explain that you have decided the time has come for change and that mealtimes will be different from now on. You might make it fun by involving your child or others in the family, in making place names or place settings, making menus or buy new (cheap) special plates, etc.

Reward your children with your attention

You may need some support to begin to enjoy being with your child at mealtimes. This is a good way to discover that your own attention is the most powerful reward you can give your young child; there is no need for sweets or treats. Being with your child and showing pleasure at their achievements will quickly show benefits.

Begin at a point where your child can achieve

It may sound odd, but you won't ever get a chance to show them how pleased you are if you set the first goal beyond their reach. For example, you start your new mealtime plan by praising your child for what they can already do, maybe telling them that they are good at eating, and you know it won't be long before they can eat more things.

Increase the goal using very gradual exposure to the types of food they currently refuse by introducing tiny amounts on the side of their plate but telling them the first goal is not for them to eat it, but to get used to it being on their plate. For example, this might be one tiny vegetable such as a pea. Or even just getting your child to touch a food they don't normally eat, which might be on your plate or a separate plate on the table.

If your child refuses to move on a step, just go back to where they are and tell them how well they are doing. For some children, just having a non-preferred food on the table is enough of a start.

To help you achieve more successful mealtime behaviour, follow this simple pathway, which uses small steps towards the eventual goal:

- Start with praise for letting the new food be nearby;

- Then on the plate;

- Then touch;

- Then lick or taste;

- Then eat;

- Then increase the quantity eaten once it is established that the new food is now on the 'nice' list;

- Give clear instructions to your child so they know the expectation. Rather than asking them if they want to try, tell them clearly what you want them to do. This isn't being strict, it is being clear. Asking a question will result in them saying 'no';

- Give your child regular opportunities to achieve the mealtime goal. So, if the goal is to increase the amount of food your child is eating, this may mean having several small mealtimes per day, rather than two or three large ones.

Also be aware of the significance of how you and your family talk about food. It is worth bearing the following tips in mind:

- Try to make positive statements about food and eating at opportunities when your child is present. You might have stopped talking about food or lost interest yourself so try to restart nice comments about food: 'This tastes really nice . . . this is my favourite . . .' etc.;

- Encourage your child to make positive statements about food and appetite, so they get used to saying words like 'yummy' or 'I'm hungry';

- Discourage scornful comments about food, especially from other children or family members;

- Discourage negative statements by your child about disliking food; say something like, 'You might not like it now, but if you keep trying, one day you will like it . . .';

• Notice your child's cues when they show they are interested in the food. Even if they do not eat it, notice when the child looks at the food, talk about it and touch it.

It is important to keep going as it may take a while to bring about a small change, and you may feel very frustrated by the slow progress and feel tempted to give up. It depends on your child's personality and their age, but pre-school children can take a week or so of repeating the same step before they make some noticeable change. Older children can take longer as they have possibly built up ideas in their head that they will find difficult to change. This may mean you need support to keep going, hence it is important for everyone in the family to agree with the plan and then stick to it consistently.

Tube Feeding

Even if your child is not being fed by a tube, the next section is worth reading as it details the planned stages to help with introducing food to a child who was not happy about eating any food at all. It demonstrates how gradual the change needs to be for some children, and that because this takes a considerable amount of time, the changes need to be planned carefully, and parents need to have support in place, in order to be able to maintain a long-term plan.

For a range of reasons, some children with physical health conditions will have required a period of time having their nutrition delivered directly into their stomach, either the whole of their nutritional needs or as top-up feeds. Usually this is from a tube fed through the nose (nasogastric) tube or a tube directly into the stomach (gastrostomy). Sometimes the medical team are satisfied that there is no longer a medical reason for the tube to remain and it is time to start eating food instead. This can cause major difficulties for some children who may have never fully experienced eating orally or developed an appetite.

It is essential that weaning a child from tube feeding should only be done with medical advice and support. These case examples show the general approach taken to tackle the weaning of a child who has been dependent on tube feeding, but if you are in this situation, talk to your medical team and dietician about how to proceed with this with your child.

Case Study – Arthur (11 months old)

Arthur was referred by his gastroenterologist because he was refusing to eat. He is aged eleven months, lives with both parents and an older sister aged three years.

Arthur was born five weeks early and was noted to have a poor suckle reflex. He refused the breast and so was bottle-fed, but this was a slow process, and he had severe reflux causing coughing and vomiting throughout the feed. He was considered to be in danger of his feed going into his airway and so the decision was taken to tube feed him until he had grown strong enough with good muscle tone for the reflux to stop.

Arthur was now at the point when he could be safely fed by mouth. However, each feed was a time-consuming process, which became increasingly anxiety-provoking and aversive for his parents as they feared he would vomit the feed. Rather than being enjoyable, feeding became an unpleasant experience for Arthur as well, with the bottle being associated with pain and vomiting. Weaning to solid foods was also started but this re-stimulated the vomiting and Arthur began to cry at the sight of the spoon.

Management of change from tube to oral feeding

The process of this change is described for Arthur:

Initial assessment

A videotape was made of a mealtime with Arthur being offered solid foods by his mum, who was the major carer. His mum had chosen appropriate food, texture, portion size and utensils for Arthur's age. She placed the bowl of food near to Arthur and he touched the food tentatively. Arthur held an empty spoon. Arthur's mother was wary of putting a spoon loaded with food to Arthur's mouth in case it stimulated vomiting. She also kept control of the bowl.

Arthur gagged when his mother loaded a spoon with food even though she had not offered it to him. It was clear that although Arthur's mother was trying hard to maintain a friendly atmosphere, the interaction was strained, and Arthur showed increasing signs of distress the longer he was sitting near the food. Children of the same age with no history of food refusal would have grabbed the bowl, touched the food, attempted to load a spoon themselves and put it to their mouths, and they may have been simultaneously chewing on some finger foods. Arthur's mum played nicely with Arthur to make him feel comfortable in the situation; she recognised when he was getting distressed with the food and spoon and moved them away.

First steps

The aims were to gain the parents' trust in the intervention, make some changes to the current mealtimes and make them pleasurable. The initial goal was to support the friendly atmosphere seen in the video assessment. Arthur's mother was given positive feedback and the psychologist acknowledged the strain of mealtimes and they discussed reasons why they were not relaxed. Arthur's mother felt that the psychologist had listened to her concerns, had an understanding of why these difficulties had developed and accepted her need for a slow pace of change. The first step in the plan was to instigate regular family mealtimes that included Arthur. Arthur was to be presented with food of a very runny texture. His parents were to show Arthur his food and to ensure they ate their food with him, showing it was enjoyable; utensils were to be present, but no spoons were loaded for Arthur.

A programme of desensitisation to solid food was initiated. This involved mum playing with the food for Arthur in the following way: puréed food was first placed on his mother's finger and dabbed around the plate and increasingly closer to Arthur, stopping at the moment he showed signs of distress. Purée was then placed on a finger food – for example, a breadstick – and again placed nearer to Arthur until he would hold the finger food himself. His mother's empty finger was then moved increasingly towards Arthur's mouth in a playful manner at a mealtime. Arthur then began to accept an empty spoon to his mouth, held by himself, then an empty spoon held by his parents. These steps took several weeks and did not progress smoothly but moved backwards and forwards depending on the emotional state of all concerned. Arthur continued to be tube fed during this time, so there were no ongoing anxieties about his nutrition.

Changes to mealtimes

Some changes began to occur during these initial stages; Arthur began to suck runny purée off his own fingers and finger foods. And he was beginning to show interest in other people eating, particularly his sister. Arthur then began accepting a spoon dipped in purée from his sister. He then began to accept a trainer beaker of water and would take about two sips per day.

The range of food that his parents had thought to offer him increased. Arthur was beginning to taste a range of foods more willingly. The next breakthrough was that Arthur allowed his mum to touch his lips with gravy on her finger. Overall, Arthur's interest in food and mealtimes and his willingness to let his mum and sister offer food without stimulating distress or vomiting increased his mum's confidence and motivated her to offer more food. The atmosphere at mealtimes became less strained and his parents even began to look forward to breakthroughs. Arthur's parents had begun to change their perception of him from non-eater (tube-reliant) to eater.

Further progress

Arthur had begun to accept minute amounts of food orally but still received all his nutrition via a tube. Arthur had not experienced feeling hungry or interest in food, although he was beginning to experience positive mealtimes. A goal now was to stimulate hunger, and this would involve reducing his tube feeds. At this stage, it was essential to consult with his gastroenterologist and dietician and to clarify a plan of action with the agreement of all concerned.

The plan was first to establish that his weight was satisfactory and there was some weight to 'play with'. In some cases, it may be necessary to increase tube feeds to put up the child's weight before any reduction can begin. Tube feeds were reduced by a small amount for two consecutive days then returned to their original amount. This pace satisfied his parent's need to maintain the weight gain that they had struggled for. Any changes in the quantity of oral food Arthur consumed were noted. Tube feeds were then reduced for longer time periods. There was an initial weight loss that his parents had been expecting, so it was easier to handle. There was a slower, but noticeable increase in Arthur's oral intake of both solid foods and water. This pattern proceeded with gradually longer periods of time with a reduction in number of tube feeds. Arthur's parents received regular support and his weight was monitored.

Final changes

Arthur began to accept thicker textures and, although vomiting occurred on occasions during this phase, it gradually reduced. Arthur began eating more finger foods that did not need much chewing. The amount he ate increased and eventually all tube feeds stopped, without him losing any weight. It took twelve months from him first being seen to the removal of the nasogastric tube, with fortnightly appointments. Arthur was then monitored much less frequently for a further year.

Eating Disorders and Disturbed Eating Attitudes and Behaviours

Case Study – Lottie (15 years old)

Lottie lives with both parents and has cystic fibrosis. Calorie intake is very important in cystic fibrosis because the body works harder to get oxygen into the bloodstream and energy is needed to fight off any infections. Lottie complained a few years ago of hating her stomach and that she didn't like having to eat high-fat foods. Lottie's rate of weight increase slowed, and it transpired that she had in mind a set weight that she would not exceed, which was considered underweight for her height.

As a consequence of her cystic fibrosis, Lottie needs to take enzymes with fat-containing foods in order to digest the fat. Otherwise she will not gain weight and could develop a serious bowel blockage. She recently became vegetarian and stopped taking her enzymes and vitamins for ethical reasons and, as a result, her weight is dropping.

Young people with physical health conditions are at risk of developing eating disorders just like their peers without physical health concerns. Additionally, there are some medical conditions that place great importance on calorie intake and most children are routinely weighed and measured at every clinic visit; this means such children may have had a greater emphasis placed on weight gain and how they look than their peers. Some conditions require medical treatment in order to gain or maintain weight and, in some instances, this can lead to problems. For example, there is a recognised form of eating disorder associated with diabetes in which young people have learned how to manipulate their insulin dose in order to control weight gain. There has been research into the rates of eating disorders developed in children and young people with physical health conditions, and while the rate of eating disorders is quite low and similar to the general population, the rates of disturbed eating behaviours or attitudes to eating are high.

Some symptoms of an eating disorder can be seen in children and young people with physical health conditions. However, typically this does not involve all the symptoms, or symptoms haven't persisted for long enough to warrant a diagnosis of an eating disorder. An eating disorder can only be diagnosed through a comprehensive assessment by an experienced mental health professional. However, it is also important to be aware of some of the ways that young people with physical health conditions might behave that could be symptoms of disturbed eating behaviours or attitudes to eating. Signs to look out for include:

- A poor appetite even when free of infection

- The avoidance of foods associated with

gastro-intestinal symptoms or a reduction in the amount of food being eaten more broadly

- The manipulation of enzyme or insulin use

- Not taking required dietary supplements or following recommendations

- Feeling full easily

- The denial of hunger

If you are concerned about your child developing an eating disorder or their attitude or behaviour to food, it is important to raise this with the team. It is usual for young people to deny they have any difficulties at first, and it can be hard for them to admit to the difficulties they are experiencing.

Returning to Lottie's case study, the team had become concerned about her weight loss and developed a plan initially with her parents, and then Lottie herself, to address this:

Plan of action for Lottie

1. A meeting with her parents and some team members, without Lottie, to acknowledge concerns over weight loss.

2. A full assessment of all the possible reasons for her poor weight gain: physical, nutritional, the amount of food eaten and psychological factors.

3. Agreement between the team and her parents to remove the focus on weight gain at clinic visits, reduce the frequency of weighing and to stop goal-setting for expected weight targets (which is common practice in medical teams).

4. The team psychologist and dietician to see Lottie alone for individual support. Areas covered included expert help on nutrition and digestion to help Lottie understand how food restriction and enzyme manipulation would impact on her body and her health, as well as a life and lifestyle assessment including teaching Lottie some cognitive behavioural techniques to help her manage worries and solve problems.

5. The gradual reintroduction of pancreatic enzymes (a gradual desensitisation approach).

6. Monitor changes in Lottie's weight and her reaction to gaining weight.

7. Work with Lottie to alter her cap on gaining weight and reduce the amount of value she was placing on her physical appearance.

Key Points

- Feeding difficulties in young children are common but can cause high levels of anxiety in parents of children with physical health conditions.

- Step-by-step approaches after a thorough assessment of where the problem lies can be effective.

- Parents need support and guidance from the healthcare team and the support of everyone at home to be able to lead on making changes.

- Children who have been tube fed can be reintroduced to oral feeding with a slow-paced, gradual approach but this MUST be done under medical guidance.

- Disturbed eating attitudes and behaviours are seen in young people with physical health conditions, particularly in the older age range. They might need specialist interventions, so it is important to ask for support and advice about how to approach them.

7

Managing Difference

This chapter is about how to build up your child's self-esteem and confidence to help them cope as they become aware of the differences between themselves and other children who don't have a physical illness. While you will learn to manage this from the time of your child's diagnosis, your child's awareness will gradually develop depending on their age and developmental stage. A baby or very young child will be completely unaware of this, and parents often comment that seeing how their child has the normal drive to develop and want to do things helps them as well, as they see how resilient their child can be, even in the face of illness.

As children get older, they do gradually become aware of any differences and begin to ask questions. For example, they may question why they have to do something such as take regular medication which their brother, sister or friend from school does not have to do. This can then lead on to a sense of unfairness or hardship, particularly if it means they can't do things their peers are doing or if they are struggling with a treatment regime. This, in turn, leads on to further questions about why they are different, and this search for a reason can lead to some difficulties with accepting why they are affected – and sometimes anger as well.

As they get older, children also tend increasingly to value the opinions of their peers. Most children want to blend in with others of their age group, to be able to do the same things as their peers and to fit in with their interests. (See Chapter 10 on adolescence and managing transition.)

This is all part of making sense of their condition, in keeping with their developmental stage or age. While this is a normal progression it can be hard to manage, as we discussed in the earlier chapter on children's understanding of illness.

A child with a long-term illness can sometimes look different from other children of a similar age as a consequence of their condition or treatment. Some of those differences will be very visible to others, such as conditions that affect the skin, or hair loss due to chemotherapy. Long-term illnesses often affect growth and can make children appear younger or smaller than their peers, and size and stature can sometimes be linked to status in childhood, so this can be a big problem for children. Other differences will be less obvious to others outside the family – for example, the need to take medication at home every day.

Case Study – Anna (5 years old)

Anna has severe eczema, which particularly affects her hands, and this is mainly treated using emollients and steroids when necessary. It is generally well controlled but can flare up from time to time. She is generally speaking an easy-going, happy child.

Although she took a while to settle into nursery, she was very happy going there and made one good friend called Laura, who moved up to reception class with her. Anna initially settled well in school but, after a few weeks, began to appear more subdued and less carefree and was occasionally tearful before going in the mornings. One day when her mother suggested Laura could come round to play, Anna got very upset and said Laura wasn't her friend any more. Laura had started to play with a new girl, Ellie, who had joined the new school with them. After a longer talk with Anna, it transpired that Laura now chose Ellie as her partner when they had to line up in pairs, because Ellie had told Laura that Anna's eczema was catching and she didn't want 'scabby' hands like Anna.

Children who look different do have to deal with comments like these, as well as the misunderstandings that underlie some of these differences. For example, once Ellie understood that Anna's eczema was not catching, and that she could in fact hold her hand safely, she was much more accepting of her.

Perhaps surprisingly, there is not always a strong link between the severity of a child's condition and the impact that it has on them psychologically. Much of how a child feels about their appearance is related to factors other than the condition itself, such as personality, resilience, confidence and support, etc. Some children who have very marked and visible differences can have the inner confidence to manage social situations well, whereas other children with only very minor noticeable differences will feel self-conscious and ashamed, which can make it hard for them to manage similar situations.

Dealing with Other People's Reactions to Your Child

If your child looks different, you will have to manage a whole range of reactions from other people, and your child will also eventually have to manage these reactions themselves. If you can develop confidence in managing them yourself, this will help your child who will pick up on your style and skills and learn from the way you approach these situations. This is not easy – so hopefully this chapter will help you feel more confident about how to manage these situations.

We live in a society that places a very high value on physical perfection and this can be difficult for anyone whose appearance does not conform to that idealised image. In addition, most of the images of 'perfection' that we are bombarded with in the media have been manipulated so that even they are not accurate representations. In this context, it can be very difficult to ensure that your child maintains a positive image of themselves as they grow up and develops a high level of self-confidence and self-esteem. We know that children who appear different will experience some name-calling and social rejection, and helping them develop a positive attitude from the start can help them deal with these situations and improve their sense of control of them.

Case Study – Olivia (newborn)

Simon and Debbie are expecting their first child together and are excited at the prospect of becoming parents. At a routine scan, they find out that their child is going to be born with a cleft lip and palate. This is a huge shock for them, because they have both been healthy and taken the usual precautions while pregnant.

After the initial upset and adjustment, they find out a lot more about the condition during the rest of the pregnancy from the antenatal team and the Cleft Lip and Palate Association (CLAPA) and so are better prepared when their daughter Olivia is born. Although they do still

find the initial time with their daughter very upsetting,
they both soon develop a very close bond with her and
feel fiercely protective towards her once they have to start
answering friends' and relatives' questions. Fortunately,
they are given lots of advice on how to manage feeding
and answer questions about the cleft from the specialist
nurses and midwives. When their daughter has the cor-
rective surgery she needs to repair her cleft, the surgery
goes well, and they are delighted with the results.

In order to help your child build confidence, you need to find a way to respond to other people's questions or comments. But in order to do that, you need to have had the opportunity to resolve some of your own feelings related to your child's appearance. This will be a gradual process and your own feelings are likely to vary but, as the above example shows, getting information and support right from the beginning can help with adjusting to your child's appearance.

However, in other situations, the child's condition will not be known before birth, and so there is no opportunity to do any preparation. The adjustment has to wait until after the child is born. Many parents are surprised that they instinctively feel a need to protect their child, and that strong protective instinct facilitates the strength needed to take on this role. However, for other parents, it can be very difficult to form a bond with a child who does not look as expected, and this can be an extremely distressing time.

As a new parent, you may need time to adapt to your child's appearance and support to deal with the emotional impact of this, in order then to be able to face the rest of the world. It can be extremely hard to manage introducing the child to family and friends when it is still upsetting for you. It is normal to feel overwhelmed by powerful emotions at times, particularly when you feel you need to protect your child from upset. It can be hard to acknowledge that you need help, as it may make you feel that you are admitting to not being good enough or not caring enough for your child. The opposite is true – by recognising that you need support, you will be in a much better position to help your child. You may find that just talking about these feelings to someone close to you is enough, but you can also speak to a member of your child's healthcare team, or your GP. There may be a helpline or resources via the patient support group for your child's condition as well.

Many parents also have to manage complicated emotions related to their own experiences of visible difference – they might have memories of being called names or being bullied at school, or even memories of taunting another child or bullying them. In addition, parents tend to start thinking about longer-term consequences immediately; for example, what will it be like when their child starts school? Will anyone ever want to go out with them? How will they ever get employed? This can build the current difficulty up into one that is much harder to tackle because it has become a huge hurdle to overcome, rather than focusing on the immediate issue the child has to manage. Children are protected from some of this because they are not able to think about the long-term difficulties in the same way, so are more able to take it one step at a time. Just knowing that your child is able to take a more short-term view can help reduce your own tendency to build the problem up in your mind.

By using the following strategies, you can help your child build their confidence by dealing with any issues as they arise and help them feel empowered to overcome difficulties when necessary.

Managing the Reactions of Others

There is a whole spectrum of responses to differences in appearance that your child may experience, ranging from 'banter' to outright social exclusion. It is sometimes difficult to know when to react and when to ignore such behaviour. There is no one 'right' way of responding to any given situation, but it can be helpful to consider various alternative approaches to take, in order to choose the most useful approach from a 'toolkit' of options in an individual situation.

Dealing with inquisitiveness or staring

Many people will take a second look or even stare at a person who looks different when they come across them by chance. Sometimes the underlying reason for this is curiosity, and there is no malicious intent behind the look. They are simply trying to make sense of what they have seen. But it is impossible for the child and parent on the receiving end to know what the intention is behind the look and, at the very least, it is confirmation that your child is different in some way.

Young children are very inquisitive by nature and when they come across something they have not experienced before, they naturally want to understand what it is. They have not yet learned any sense of social restraint, so they will ask very directly or comment spontaneously and this can be done quite innocently without intending to cause any hurt. For example, they may say something like, 'Why is your skin red and bumpy?' or 'Ugh . . . why do you have that tube in your nose?'

In most situations, it is best to have a tried and tested response that includes first a simple explanation, and then something to reassure the young child. For example, you may say, 'He has a skin condition called eczema, but don't worry, it's not catching . . .' or 'She has an illness called cancer and the treatment meant she couldn't eat for a while but now she is getting better.' It can then help to redirect the conversation on to something completely different to distract the child and to continue in a more normal conversation: 'I like your trainers – I really like that colour – where did you get them from?'

It can also help to use humour to try and take the tension out of the situation – but it can be hard to think of the right comment at the time you need it! It is hard to be prescriptive about this – it has to fit in with the individual's style and context and can be thought of as part of the 'toolkit' you or your child can draw on in these circumstances.

When dealing with older children or adults in these situations, it is worth remembering that sometimes people feel awkward or embarrassed by their own reactions to someone who appears different. In these situations, it is possible to overcome this by taking a lead in the conversation and bringing up another topic that feels more comfortable for both parties. This helps defuse any embarrassment but also helps the receiver see that appearances can be deceptive and that you and your child are able to manage social situations.

However, it can also be important to go one step further and help them learn that their comments might upset or embarrass another child. For example, you can say, 'She has a tube to take food into her tummy because she can't eat at the moment. She doesn't like it when people say things about it because it hurts her feelings.'

This can also be a helpful approach to take with adults who are looking inquisitive but don't actually say anything. For example, you can say, 'You seem to be wondering what is wrong with her. She had to have surgery on her face but she's recovering now. Please don't stare at her because it makes her feel self-conscious.'

Despite this, there is no doubt that there will be times when either a child or their parent feels worn down by being the one who has to take a positive approach, and especially if they are feeling sensitive or less resourceful for other reasons. We are still a very 'beauty' dominated society and it is hard growing up in that sort or culture when we don't fit that 'norm'. It is normal to lose your temper sometimes when someone is staring or making a comment – they are certainly likely to remember it and hopefully think twice next time they are faced with a similar situation!

Dealing with bullying

All schools have to have an anti-bullying policy and also go beyond this to promote methods of preventing a bullying culture from developing. In the past, the focus has often been on taking an individual approach to resolving difficulties between the 'bully' and the 'victim'. However, it has been found to be much more successful to take a whole-class approach, developing a shared value of respect for all, and creating a culture of high standards that also encourages all children to challenge name-calling or bullying that they witness. If this approach is taken, then it is not just children who look different who should benefit: it is *all* children. This approach can help counterbalance any power imbalance, which can make it hard for individual children to stand up for themselves in a situation when they are faced with a child who is older or more popular than they are.

Case Study – Daniel (9 years old)

Daniel is quite small for his age and has had to miss quite a lot of school for medical treatment. He returns to school after a week's absence and one of the other boys in the year above asks if he has been skiving. When Dan says he has been unwell, the older boy then tells some of the others to keep away from Dan because 'it's catching'. They play a game throughout break that involves avoiding Dan as he runs around the playground, as if he is contaminated. Dan is upset but plays along.

At lunchtime, when Dan sits down, the other boy makes a big show of avoiding sitting anywhere near him and encourages his friends to do the same. Another boy, who is one of the taller and 'cooler' boys, bravely decides to take them on, and sits next to Dan. Dan is pleased and the other boy talks to him normally. After lunch when they all go out to play, the other boy tells the playground supervisor what had been happening and she tells them all to play together. They are all soon running around together.

Children with a long-term illness may also end up missing school more frequently than healthy children, because of ill health or hospital appointments and treatments. Missing school means not only do they have work to catch up on, but they will also have missed out on social opportunities with their peer group. It can be very daunting for a child who has missed school to return, and they may be reluctant to do so. They often face questions about why they were off and may find that friendship groups have moved on. It can be helpful to think about this with your child when they return, so that they have an explanation ready. (There are also more strategies for helping your child in this situation in Chapter 8 about school and education.)

If you are concerned your child is being bullied, it is not always easy to find out exactly what is happening – your child may be reluctant to tell you, or they may find it too painful to admit it to you. It is important to talk to their teacher, who needs to know your concerns in order to deal with it effectively. Any bullying should be dealt with in the early stages, and in a way that doesn't mean the victim ends up feeling worse; otherwise it will eat away at your child's self-confidence. If the school has successfully developed a culture of inclusion and valuing difference, then these difficulties can be addressed as part of that agenda, so that the child doing the bullying is not seen as the 'stronger' one, but the one whose behaviour has to change.

In some situations, it can also be difficult for a child who looks 'normal' but who can't participate in 'normal' activities because of the restrictions due to their physical illness. For example, if a child has a complex treatment regime, it is much harder for them to go on sleepovers or trips away with friends or school. These types of 'invisible' differences can make it hard precisely because the child's expectations are that they are 'normal', and they don't want to have to make allowances for their condition. Occasionally, there will also be situations where their illness gets challenged or someone questions why they need additional support or special treatment.

Sharing Information and Managing Transition to Secondary School

Case Study – Tariq (10 years old)

Tariq was treated for a cancerous tumour when he was seven years old. He had surgery, followed by chemotherapy and radiotherapy and has now been cancer-free for nearly four years. During this time, he has been well supported by his small primary school, where he is well known, and he has mostly enjoyed his time at school. Despite having to miss quite a lot of school, he settled back in well, is confident socially and has caught up with the education he missed. He is small for his age and is being treated with a growth hormone replacement. He is due to transition to secondary school in September. The secondary school most people from his primary school go to is very large but nearby, and has a very good reputation for achievement.

Having been to visit the new school, Tariq is now wor-
ried about how he will fit in since he will be one of the
youngest and probably the smallest. However, he is clear
he doesn't want everyone to know he has had cancer. His
parents are also unsure about what to tell his new school
about his previous treatment.

There is a balance between maintaining privacy or confidentiality and letting other people know about your child's
condition. There are some situations when it is important
for others to know, in order to ensure that your child is safe
and cared for properly. It is also a way of ensuring that your
child gets any additional treatment or support they need
at school. However, once the information becomes widely
known, it can be hard to control how it is used, and while
most children and parents would treat it respectfully, others
can use it in a way that will cause your child to be upset.

This is especially the case for some conditions, such as
HIV infection, which still carry considerable stigma, and
if this becomes well known it can be very difficult for a
child to manage the consequences. In these circumstances,
it is usually best to wait until the child has had the chance
to have some preparation themselves, and can understand
the implications of disclosure before encouraging them
to share information. Even when children are aware of
their diagnosis, it is often helpful to say something like,
'Although you had cancer, that isn't the most important
thing about you. The most important things are what make

you the boy/girl you are. Let's think about all the great things that make you, you.'

In Tariq's case, it would be very important for his parents to let the new school know about his previous health problems and to let them know he is still being monitored for any late effects of his treatment and will need to go to some hospital appointments. It would also be helpful for the Special Educational Needs Co-ordinator (SENCO) at the school to know about the possible impact on his growth, so that he/she understands that this may be an issue for Tariq. There are some very helpful leaflets written for teachers to help them understand the impact of cancer treatment on children, which can provide some background information (see Resources section at the end of the book). However, there is not necessarily a need for all the other children to know about Tariq's condition, so he can decide for himself whether or not he lets his new friends know about his treatment.

Dealing with Cyberbullying

The development of cyberbullying has caused a huge amount of concern, partly because it is so much harder for parents to know what is happening, and partly because, by its very nature, it is so much more 'public' than bullying face-to-face. Responses can easily be seen by hundreds or even thousands of other young people, so the shame felt by the 'victim' is that much greater. Hiding behind the anonymity of online postings also means that some people feel much more able to say shocking things – things they would not dare to say face-to-face.

Case Study – Carol (15 years old)

Carol is fifteen and has always been self-conscious because of a scar that she has on her chest as a result of cardiac surgery. A group of her friends at school are sharing selfies of themselves in low-cut tops, showing off their cleavage. They are daring each other to send the images to the boys in their class to see how many 'likes' they get. Carol posts a picture of herself in which a corner of her scar is visible but which she feels looks pretty good. Only a few of her friends 'like' her picture and she feels mortified. She feels even worse when a 'friend' comments on the picture saying he would not want to touch her.

It is really important for young people to know about the dangers of cyberbullying and sharing information online. If this is done from an early age when parents have some control over access to online material, then hopefully children grow up with some awareness of these issues.

However, it is much harder with older children to manage their time online. They can become preoccupied with what other people are thinking and doing in a way that is really unhelpful and undermines their self-confidence. However, it is hard to protect them from this when it is what everyone else is doing.

It can be helpful to set some limits: for example, by limiting online access after a certain time in the evening and during shared times, such as while eating or doing a family activity. It is also important to make sure your child knows they should not make themselves vulnerable to such bullying by revealing too much information about themselves to people they don't know well. This includes revealing publicly identifiable information about or images of themselves that could be misused.

If you find out that something upsetting or offensive has been posted about your child, you should make sure they keep the evidence and then report this to their service provider. It is worth encouraging your child to look at the resources on websites such as bullying.co.uk or kidscape.org that help support them to be safe online, but also encourage them to seek help when necessary (see Resources section at the end of the book).

Ways of Building Your Child's Self-esteem

As well as managing any difficult situations that arise, it is also worth taking a proactive approach to help build your child's self-esteem. If they feel good about themselves and recognise their own skills and strengths, then this will be a protective factor for the times when they face challenges. It is easiest to do this by encouraging them to develop skills in an area that interests them and where there is potential for them to participate and enjoy themselves.

Make sure your child grows up with a healthy cynicism for the 'beauty myth' that is in popular culture. For example, point out when you see celebrities with 'perfect' skin that this is an airbrushed image, not a real image. Make them aware that it is not possible for everyone to be super skinny and that many of the people who are that thin are actually very unhealthy. However, don't avoid talking about appearance completely. It is still important for them to think about their appearance, and to make an effort to look good, e.g., by choosing to wear flattering colours. Make sure to pay them a compliment when they do look good.

All of us have to learn to identify and make the most of our strengths, and the same principle should apply to children with a long-term illness. Help your child by noticing when they do something well and support them in making progress with it – remember to start from where they are already and build on small achievable steps. Make goals based on them as individuals rather than necessarily trying to win or be the best at something. Notice when they do something well and praise them for the effort they put in, rather than just the result. It can be a great achievement to participate in an event – they don't have to win for it to be a success. Tell other people about what they are doing well – for example, their teacher or other members of the family – so that their progress is recognised and celebrated.

Try not to be negative or criticise when things go wrong – it is a helpful life skill to accept you have to make mistakes in order to learn from them! Instead, help them to problem solve by taking the role of a 'coach' and help them to think through what they could do differently next time. It is tempting as a parent to point out what went wrong and tell them what they should do. Instead of doing this, try and get them to tell you what happened and ask open questions such as:

- How do you think that went?

- What did you feel went well?

- What sort of things that you said or did do you now wish you had done differently?

- What would help you next time to do it that way?

- What would you like me to do to help with that?

By stepping back yourself and encouraging your child to think through the steps rather than just giving them the answers, this will help them to adopt a problem-solving approach and help them to feel confident to overcome minor setbacks.

Developing Confidence in Social Situations

Helping your child to become more assertive and take some control in social situations is a really useful skill to learn.

This is something that many children and adults who lack confidence actively avoid, but it is only by practising and overcoming some of these fears that they can develop the skills needed to manage social situations. Often, parents find their own self-confidence improves when they see their child acting assertively with friends. Sometimes, supporting your child can benefit you. Withdrawing eats away at confidence, and especially during childhood when other children and young people are gradually getting better at developing these skills.

Case Study – Rylan (12 years old)

Rylan was born with a heart defect. Throughout his childhood, he has had several operations and admissions to hospital. He takes daily medications and will continue to have regular check-ups. He is small for his age and, because he has missed quite a lot of school, he doesn't always get good marks and has to attend catch-up groups at lunchtime. He lives with his mum, Janine.

Janine is not a confident person and doesn't have a lot of friends. She says that Rylan is like her in that he is shy. Rylan is getting worried that he doesn't have any friends and because he goes to hospital a lot, he thinks the other kids won't like him very much. Rylan is starting not to want to attend school and never goes out after he has come home in the evening. Janine is OK with that as she says they like each other's company. It is important, though, that Rylan is listened to, as he is worried about friendships and school is becoming a place he is concerned about. It would now be helpful for Janine and Rylan to develop a plan to help him to continue to attend school rather than withdrawing to the comfort zone of home.

Rylan and Janine undertake an activity on paper, drawing out where Rylan is now, where he wants to get to and what is in the way of getting there. Rylan says he wants to picture it as standing on one side of the river with all the kids playing together on the other side; he wants to get to the other side and join in. Rylan and his mum work out that he needs to cross the river on stepping stones. He decides that each stepping stone earns him 100 points and when he gets to 500 points he is on the other side.

They work out what he needs to do to earn his first 100 points and, as can be seen in the diagram, they break each step down into a small manageable task.

Every day his mum asks Rylan how he is doing and supports him by awarding the 100 points when he has achieved his stepping stone. Doing this together means that she is involved and also benefitting from his increased self-confidence.

Figure 5 – Rylan's Stepping Stones

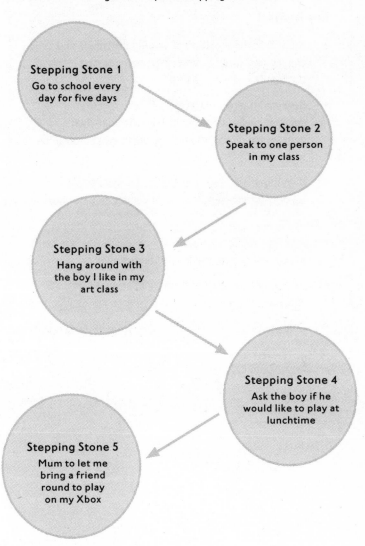

Stepping Stone 1
Go to school every day for five days

Stepping Stone 2
Speak to one person in my class

Stepping Stone 3
Hang around with the boy I like in my art class

Stepping Stone 4
Ask the boy if he would like to play at lunchtime

Stepping Stone 5
Mum to let me bring a friend round to play on my Xbox

Key Points

- Actively foster a culture of valuing difference and challenging society's unrealistic perfectionist ideals in the family.

- Develop a range of strategies for the spectrum of comments your child might receive about their appearance or condition – talk about what works/ what doesn't.

- If you find this very upsetting, it can help to get support for yourself in order to be able to help your child.

- Take a proactive approach with school – stay one step ahead and control the flow of information.

- Help your child develop an area of strength they can enjoy and feel proud about.

- Help your child to stay safe online from an early age.

8

School and Education

Children spend more than 1,000 hours in school each academic year, which is more than 12,000 hours over their childhood and teenage years – so school is an important part of a child's life. As well as providing education and teaching new skills, schools provide the opportunity for children to develop socially, and help them to learn independence out of the home setting. It can also help them to develop new areas of skill that can boost their self-esteem and get a sense of belonging from being part of a wider community. Going to school can be particularly important for children with a long-term illness because it is the part of their world that is 'normal', where they can just be 'children' and take part in activities that all children their age are doing.

In principle, children with a medical condition should have the same rights to a good education as other children, including going on educational trips, taking part in sports and PE. But, in reality, they can experience difficulties with accessing all areas of the curriculum and maintaining continuity at school, academically and socially. Depending on their condition, children may have to miss school due to ill health or medical appointments and this makes it harder for them to keep up with academic work and with their social groups.

In addition, there are some medical conditions that directly involve the brain (such as epilepsy or a brain tumour) which are known to make it more likely that a child will develop either specific or general learning difficulties. There are also some treatments that may affect learning and development (such as radiotherapy for some cancers) and affected children may need additional support with learning in order to achieve their full potential. Support should be provided within the education system, usually within mainstream education but, in some cases, a child's needs can be better met with more specialist provision.

Unfortunately, parents often report that they are not able to get the help that they feel their child needs in school, and find it challenging to argue for extra support. Many parents find the prospect of talking to teachers quite daunting, let alone headteachers (it can make them feel that they themselves are back in school and about to be told off!). Also, teachers and schools only have access to finite resources so there is a limit to what teachers and schools can provide. There is also lot of variation in how well they are able to provide for each individual child's needs. Schools are all monitored closely, and teachers often report feeling overwhelmed by all the demands placed on them, and it can be hard for them to have the flexibility in their schedule to allow them to make adaptations to meet individual needs.

There is a statutory guidance document about support for children with a medical difficulty in school called *Supporting Pupils at School with Medical Conditions*, issued in December 2015, and this can be accessed via the website listed in the Resources section at the end of the book. This gives very clear guidance that pupils at school with medical conditions should be properly supported so that they have full access to education, including school trips and physical education. This is done by setting up an Individual Healthcare Plan (IHP) in partnership with parents, the school and the child's support services. The plan should include what additional help the child may need in school, and who is going to provide it.

All schools have a SENCO who is responsible for implementing the school's policy regarding children with additional needs. Your child's class teacher will probably be the teacher who knows your child best, but the SENCO will also be the 'go to' person to communicate with if you have any concerns about your child's access to education. They will be able to assess whether they need any additional support in school and they can help draw up an IHP for your child.

The example IHP shown here is for Jake who has a nut allergy and is in primary school, just starting Year 3.

Individual Health Plan – Greenview Primary School

Jake Smith (7 years 8 months)

Class: 3W

Drawn up by Jake's mother, Mrs Alison Smith and
Miss Wheeler, class teacher

Date to review: Within one year

Describe medical needs and give details of child's symptoms, treatments, and any equipment	Jake has a serious, life-threatening allergy to peanuts and cashews. He therefore has to avoid these nuts at all times.
	Jake develops symptoms within a few minutes of contact with nuts. His symptoms include wheezing, difficulty breathing, feeling light-headed, swelling of his lips, tongue and face or raised itchy swellings anywhere on his body. He may feel frightened and panicky and should be given reassurance.
	If Jake shows any signs of difficulty breathing, he must immediately be treated using the EpiPen® provided (see below).
Name of medication, dose, method of administration details	EpiPen® auto injector – two are provided.
	The EpiPen® should be injected into his outer thigh, as instructed on the packaging. If there is no improvement after ten minutes, the second EpiPen® can be given.
	An ambulance must be called immediately – dial 999.
	Jake should lie down and, if he feels faint, his feet and legs should be raised.

| Arrangements for school visits/trips etc. | The EpiPen® needs to be taken whenever Jake is off site, even if he is not expected to eat while on the trip.

The EpiPen® should be carried by a member of staff who has received the appropriate training to use it. |
| --- | --- |
| Staff training needed/ undertaken – who, what, when | Jake's class teacher and at least two other members of staff need to have training in how and when to use the EpiPen®. This training should be given on a yearly basis.

Given the school is likely to have other children with an allergy in its care, it is advisable for more than this number to have training.

The training will be provided by the local community nursing team. Additional information can be given by Jake's mother and father. |
| Details of who to contact | Jake's mother Alison Smith [mobile number]

Jake's father Harry Smith [mobile number] |

The above information is, to the best of my knowledge, accurate at the time of writing and I give consent to school/setting staff administering medicine in accordance with the school/setting policy. I will inform the school/setting immediately, in writing, if there is any change in dosage or frequency of the medication or if the medicine is stopped.

Signature of parent(s)   Date

Communication with School

Starting school is a very significant milestone for any child and there are other important transitions, particularly junior to senior school, where you may need to do some preparation to help the school understand what your child needs and explain about their medical condition.

There is a balance between maintaining some privacy for your child and how much information teachers and other children should have. It is usually best to start from a 'need to know' basis. The teacher and school do need to know how to manage your child's condition in order to keep them safe at school, so they do need to know about any monitoring or medication that your child may need when they are in school. It can also be helpful for them to know about any forthcoming procedures that may affect your child, both in terms of managing their absence in school, but also in terms of the impact this may have on the child beforehand or afterwards. This can help them plan the best resources for your child while they are away. For example, when children are in hospital, they should have access to education via hospital school education services and, if they have significant absences from school, they can receive home tutoring. Creative use of the Internet and facilities such as Skype can also help children continue to feel connected to their class and peers during absences.

Other children in the class may need to know something about your child's condition if it is going to affect them or in order for them to best understand your child and accept them as a peer. For example, if your child has had treatment that has made it more difficult for them to do the things they used to be able to do, this may need to be explained to other children so that they can understand and make allowances. They may need reassurance about the changes and ideas about how to help the child join in activities again. This is sometimes best done just before the child returns to the classroom, so that any strategies are already in place to welcome the child back. If you have had a discussion with your child's teacher so they know what to expect, he or she can then help the rest of the class prepare for this.

Schools may also benefit from further training or information about supporting a child with particular medical conditions. Many of the charities produce leaflets or guides to help explain a condition to other children; for example, the Children's Cancer and Leukaemia Group (CCLG) booklet *Welcome Back! A Guide for Teachers Helping Children and Young People Returning to School after Cancer*, and the National Eczema Society leaflet *All about Eczema – An Information Pack for Schools*. Links to the websites to access these leaflets are provided in the Resources section of this book. These resources will often provide the sort of information the school needs about the child's condition but may also suggest some educational activities for children that might help.

Transition into School from Nursery to Mainstream Reception Class

Many parents worry about their children starting in reception class at primary school. It is not just about your child entering 'big school' but also a developmental marker in your life as well as your child's – going to school is a first step into the outside world. Your child might have been to a nursery or pre-school already; if this is attached to the mainstream school then the transition might be slightly easier in that the location, environment and faces are already familiar. If the school is entirely new, then it takes a bit of time for you and your child to get used to the new place and people, so don't be hard on yourself and expect it to all run smoothly from day one. The key to transitions of any sort is to understand that it is a process of change, not a one-off event.

The transition phase should ideally begin before the actual move. For parents of a child with a long-term health condition, the first step will be to think about which is the best school to manage your child's medical condition. If there is a particular school that you think meets your child's needs, medical teams will often help with school applications. However, it is often difficult to make a final decision on a school before your child has begun there, so don't be too quick to write off a school as it might end up suiting your child very well. Most school teachers are more than happy to meet parents beforehand to talk about meeting needs and any reasonable adjustments that could be made.

Some medical teams will also visit the school with you and help to write an Individual Healthcare Plan. Depending on your child's healthcare needs, you may choose not to disclose the diagnosis to other parents. Remember that the teachers will maintain confidentiality and so will only tell other people if you have agreed to this beforehand. With your child's class teacher, agree some means of regular communication and updates so you feel you have contact but are not overly intrusive.

Transition to Secondary School

Transition to secondary school can be particularly challenging. A child who has become confident at a small primary school where they are well known and one of the oldest pupils will find that they are one of the youngest in a secondary school and have to re-establish themselves there.

Secondary schools are very aware of how important a smooth transition from primary to secondary school is, and they usually arrange visits and activities for children in their last term of primary school to ease this process. They may invite children to the new school for an introductory morning or day, and familiarise them with the key people they may meet as well as the expectations the school will have. For example, the most common fear that children express about their move to secondary school is that they will get lost and not be able to find their way. Many schools manage this by gradually introducing children to the new site, and also by giving them strategies to manage this fear by talking to them about how they can ask for help or where they can get help with this. In fact, hardly any children do get lost and, if they do, they learn how to find their way, which is a useful skill in itself. For children with a medical condition and any other child who has had contact with the school SENCO, the SENCO from the primary school will usually arrange a handover to the new SENCO to make sure that key information is successfully communicated.

Case Study – Salim (11 years old)

Salim is about to move to secondary school. Some, but not all, of his friends from primary school are going to the same school. Salim has diabetes and needs to monitor his blood sugar and have insulin injections during the school day. He also has some restrictions on the food and drink he can have at school.

At his primary school, most of Salim's friends knew of his medical condition and had got used to it. He had teachers who would look after him, make sure his treatments were done and phone his mum if he was unwell.

Salim's mother is worried that Salim will forget his treatment routine and be tempted to eat or drink food from the other children because he won't want to tell them he has diabetes. She is also worried that the teachers are too busy, and the school is too big to take good care of him. Salim's biggest worry is that he will get lost.

Salim's mother was very pleased that the school told her about the Individual Healthcare Plan and allowed the Clinical Nurse Specialist for his diabetes team to go to school with her to write and agree the plan. Mum started to allow Salim to help out more with his treatments at home rather than doing it all for him, so she could be reassured that he did know what needed to be done and when. Salim was pleased that some of his old friends were going to the school with him as that made him feel like he had some allies.

After the end of the first term, when Salim was asked about how he had settled into school, he could not remember ever being nervous. He had made lots of new friends and had told some of them about his diabetes. Although not all the teachers knew about his diabetes, his form tutor and the SENCO were around to help if he needed it. And he had never once got lost.

Developing a Good Relationship with School

Given how much time a child has in school, it is important to feel you can trust your child's teacher and school and it is worth investing time in supporting the school. Many parents find the prospect of talking to teachers quite daunting, and this is made even more difficult if you are talking to them about concerns about your child, which can make you feel more emotional yourself, or feel defensive about them. Try and go to all the parent–teacher meetings you are invited to and find out about topics that your child is learning about, so you can contribute as much as possible.

If you are concerned about something that is happening at school, ask your child's teacher for a meeting and consider whether it would be helpful to include the SENCO. It can be very hard to know what is happening day-to-day in school and therefore it is best to go in with an open mind and focus on problem-solving rather than blame. Typically, teachers are more than happy to have regular communication with parents. Teachers are experts in education and child development and behaviour but not experts in your child's medical condition. They are often reassured by regular update meetings and working together with parents. This is usually better than staying away and only going in when there is a problem. Don't feel like you are making a nuisance of yourself; offer it right at the beginning: 'Would it be helpful if I had a ten-minute update meeting with you once every half term or more frequently if there is a need?'

Dealing with Protecting Your Child – Managing Your Anxiety and Minimising Their Anxiety

Many parents find it difficult to know how much to trust the school to keep their child safe, and it can be hard to feel confident that a school can take care of an individual child's needs in the context of a busy classroom. However, it helps a lot if you can have a plan which has been agreed with the school, so that they are clear about what your child's needs are and you know that they have an action plan in place.

At times, children may lose their confidence and, if they have missed school for a period of time, they often find it hard to return. It can sometimes be genuinely hard to know whether to encourage a child to return to school who says they are feeling unwell and tired to 'have a go', or whether to give them a break and keep them at home. When children (and adults!) feel anxious, the natural response is to avoid whatever it is that makes them anxious, but this can sometimes result in making it even harder eventually to face the problem. As we all know, anticipatory anxiety can mislead you into thinking you really should not do something, when actually it is not nearly as bad as you thought it was going to be once you actually do it. Think how many times you have dreaded something but then found it wasn't anywhere near as bad as you predicted. Often, it is not so much that a child is being manipulative and deliberately misleading – they are really convinced that it will make them feel worse.

On the other hand, if you over-protect your child and keep them away from school when they could have managed and would have felt better once there, they will never have the experience of seeing that actually it was not as bad as they had expected, and also not have the chance to learn to manage this sort of uncertainty. This could reduce their chances of developing new skills and having new experiences, and they will pick up from you that schools are dangerous places – which is not what you want them to believe.

Case Study – Andrew (7 years old)

Andrew had a lot of infections in his early childhood, so he missed a lot of days at nursery and, when it came to starting at primary school, he developed lung disease, which gradually deteriorated. He missed about a third of reception and Year 1 due to ill health and repeated hospital admissions. Unfortunately, towards the end of Year 1, he was involved in an accident out of school which resulted in a small fracture to his arm. Following this incident, he struggled to return to school.

He was then admitted to hospital following another lung infection and it took him nearly six weeks to fully recover. By then he was due to be in Year 2 but had spent less than a year in full-time school in total. He was behind in both literacy and numeracy, and did not have any friendship groups within school.

Both Andrew and his mother, Jane, were extremely anxious about him returning to school. Jane had reservations about allowing him to attend in the autumn/winter because of the higher risk of infection and wanted to wait until spring. However, his medical team advised he was well enough to return, so he was not eligible for home tuition.

A very gradual return-to-school plan was developed in conjunction with his class teacher, Andrew and his mother. They were able to identify particular times when he felt very anxious (for example, going into the playground in the morning with everyone rushing around or during playtime in boisterous games) and find ways to manage these situations. His mother was initially allowed to bring Andrew straight into the classroom, rather than having to manage the busy playground before school. During breaks, Andrew's teacher chose a 'buddy' to be with Andrew each day, so he had someone with him while he got to know the other children better.

Both Andrew and his mother needed support from a psychologist to manage the anxiety that they felt during this return to school, but he did successfully reintegrate. He did need some additional support to help him catch up with the school work he had missed as well, but this was done within a small group in the classroom, so he was gradually able to reintegrate with his peer group.

Accessing Further Support for Children with Special Educational Needs

Some children do have physical or learning disabilities directly related to their medical condition, or to the treatment for it. Some of these children may be eligible for what is known as an 'Education, Health and Care' plan (EHC). EHC plans have been introduced as part of the new Special Educational Needs and Disability (SEND) Code of Practice published in 2015 and are gradually replacing the previous system of Statements of Special Educational Needs.

The definition of disability includes a 'physical or mental impairment which has a long-term and substantial adverse effect on their ability to carry out normal day-to-day activities (Equality Act 2010)'. And a learning difficulty is defined as having a 'significantly greater difficulty in learning than the majority of others of the same age' (see Resources section for further information about special educational needs).

This system aims to ensure that support is planned in a 'joined up' way between education, health and social care and to ensure this is a collaborative process involving parents and children themselves whenever possible. The emphasis is on a more streamlined and briefer assessment process; for example, the local authority has up to six weeks from request to agree an assessment and then the assessment has to be completed within twenty weeks. The plans should explicitly identify outcomes that should be achieved, rather than the previous system of identifying support that will be provided. For example, the plan may include outcomes such as 'Sara will increase her social contact with her peers by spending a part of her free playtime each day with another nominated child'. There is also the option for parents to have more control of how the budget is spent and to be involved in developing the right sort of provision for their child.

If you feel your child needs additional support in school due to a disability or special educational needs, first discuss this with your child's teacher and SENCO. It is worth knowing there are free, impartial and confidential services to support parents with children with special educational needs and disability called Information, Advice and Support (IAS) Services, which were previously known as Parent Partnership Services (PPS). IAS Services are funded by their local authority; however, they are all expected to be at 'arm's length' of the local authority and to provide impartial information, advice and support (see Resources section for contact details).

Remember, it is not necessary for the child to have an EHC plan in order to get some support in school – many needs can be met without an EHC plan. It is more important to focus on getting the sort of support that will help them to make progress in the school setting, rather than thinking you must have an EHC.

Case Study – Amal (14 years old)

Amal had a brain tumour when she was very young and had to have surgery as well as radiotherapy to treat this. The cancer has been cured but she has experienced some late effects of the treatment and now needs hormonal treatment. She is now fourteen and in Year 9 at school. Her parents feel that she is not learning as well as her older sister did at that age and they are concerned that this may be because of the cancer and treatment.

In particular, she seems to struggle to remember what she has learned and often appears to drift off and lose her concentration. She is quite conscientious and appears to try hard at school, including doing her homework, but her achievement levels are at the lower end of the range for her age. An assessment was carried out by an educational psychologist, who found Amal was achieving at about the right level for her own abilities, even though this was lower than her sister, who happened to be very able. She was able to make recommendations about how to develop Amal's study skills, using a more structured approach to revision. She showed Amal how to draw up a revision timetable in which specific topics were allocated to relatively brief revision slots and, at the end of each session, Amal completed exam questions related to this topic. By focusing on a topic and actively testing her own knowledge as she progressed, Amal used her revision time much more effectively. This helped Amal feel more supported and confident for her GCSEs.

Key Points

- School is very important for children but, for a child with a medical condition, it can be harder to access all the benefits of school.

- It is natural to want to protect your child when they start or change schools – you may need to manage your own anxiety in order to prevent your child becoming anxious, too.

- Develop a good relationship with school by attending any meetings about your child and checking with their teacher the best way of communicating with them.

- Peer relationships are very important to children – help them manage difference to help them feel included and 'normal'.

- Times of transitions can be particularly difficult for children – remember, this is a process rather than a one-off event.

9

Caring for Siblings

It is difficult enough to manage differences between siblings when you have two or more children in the family, but this becomes even harder when you have a child with a long-term illness. Caring for a child with a long-term illness usually involves additional demands on your resources, both practical and emotional, and this can have a knock-on effect on other children in the family. All siblings have slightly different needs, so you have to adjust your parenting style to manage these differences, but it is particularly difficult to juggle responding to the needs of your well child or children when the needs of an unwell child may sometimes have to take priority.

Most parents start with the ideal of wanting to be able to share out their attention or love equally between siblings and trying to be fair to each child. Many adults can recall situations from their own childhood when they felt a parent showed favouritism and times when they competed fiercely with their brother or sister for their parent's attention. This sort of rivalry can be very intense, so parents often do their best to try and prevent it from happening with their own children. But if one of your children does have a higher level of dependency on you because of their illness, then they will need a greater share of the care you can provide, and this can be difficult to manage within a family. All your children will want your attention, and well siblings don't always understand why they are not being put first.

The realisation that you cannot meet the needs of one child, because you are already occupied with your unwell child who has to take priority, can cause a tremendous amount of guilt. While rationally you know you can't be in two places at once, this sense of being 'torn in half' can be hard emotionally. If one of your own children accuses you of giving your unwell child more attention than them or neglecting them, this can be very hurtful.

Although it is important to try and recognise the needs of well siblings as much as you can, this chapter is not intended to make you feel guilty about how siblings may be affected; it is intended to help you find some ways to do the best you can, under the circumstances, and to help you to feel a sense of satisfaction that you are a 'good enough' parent. Almost all parents strive for perfection despite this being an impossible goal. Parents of children with a long-term illness often have to strive more than other parents because of the physical and emotional demands that the illness places on them. So, for that reason, parents of children with a long-term illness should be supported to feel a sense of personal achievement – you really do go that extra mile.

Young Children – The Impact of Separation

The impact of living with a sibling with a physical health condition will depend on the age and developmental stage of a well child. Very young children will particularly miss the physical presence of a parent, and find separations (for example, for hospital stays) very difficult. It is harder for them to understand timescales, so it can be more difficult to explain to them and be able to reassure them about when you will be back.

Try to ensure the sibling has a familiar routine and regular substitute carers if you are not able to be there. Routines help provide some security in the face of other things that can't be controlled. If you have family members who can step in as carers, this can be very helpful especially if they are able to come and stay at your home so that they fit into the sibling's normal routine. Many other people – for example, your friends or parents of your children's friends – enjoy being able to offer help in this situation, so although it sometimes feels uncomfortable to ask for help, remember that some people might actually be very happy to provide this. For example, arranging an afternoon with a close friend's family can actually be a great way of both distracting your child and helping them to have a positive time, even if you can't be there yourself.

If the child is old enough, you can prepare them for any planned admissions or absences by using a visual calendar to help them understand what will be happening and who will be looking after them. They may find it hard to hold in mind what is happening each day and how long the separation will be, but seeing it in pictures will help them to make sense of any separation. See example on page 179.

Remember that while children are very young, they do accept things as normal if they are normal in their family. If something happens consistently, such as their brother or sister's regular treatment regime, then that does seem normal to them and they will accept it as part of their day-to-day life. At a young age, they are not able to make comparisons and therefore don't realise that this is unusual. Only later, once they are at school and get used to visiting other families, do they begin to realise that this may be unusual compared to other children or families.

One strategy that some parents find helpful as a means of sharing out attention is to have a regular play session focused on your well child or children; for example, playing something they have chosen. It is often suggested that this should be fifteen minutes a day, but this may be hard to achieve. Even if you can't spend as much time as that with each child, it is helpful to spend a few minutes each day or a longer session two or three times a week. It is not just the amount of time you spend with them that is important, it is having the focus just on them, and on making this 'their' time to choose what they want to do. You don't necessarily have to do a special activity – just cuddling up together looking at a picture book is fine. You may find that initially it is hard for the child to end these sessions, and they become upset or plead for more time, but once you

Example of calendar:

Monday 6th	Tuesday 7th	Wednesday 8th	Thursday 9th	Friday 10th
Mum and Sam into hospital	To Sarah's: Dad to pick up	Mum pick up	Grandma	Mum

Monday 13th	Tuesday 14th	Wednesday 15th	Thursday 16th	Friday 17th
Dad picking up	Grandma	Mum and Sam back home!		

have got a routine, then they will get used to the idea of 'their' time and you can both enjoy it.

Older Children – Staying in Touch

As children get older, even if they can manage without you there physically temporarily, they will miss your attention and interest because they want to share their world with you; for example, they will want to tell you about what is happening at school or show you new skills they have learned.

As they get older, find ways of keeping each other updated, preferably in a format the sibling uses anyway; for example, via Skype or Facetime, or by sharing messages such as on a family WhatsApp group. This is a way of keeping your child in mind even if you can't physically be there, by showing you know about what they are doing and care about how it is going. If you find you need to, set reminders on your phone to contact them. Although they may not respond, they will know you have thought about them. This way, a regular catch-up time becomes part of the routine, in the same way as a play session does for younger children.

There can be additional challenges in how older children deal with having a sibling with a long-term illness. As peer relationships become more highly valued, they may increasingly want to be similar to their peers and may begin to resent any differences that they perceive as unfair.

They will also begin to realise that their brother or sister is different and will usually ask more questions about why this is, or why they need the treatment that they do. This can also lead to more situations in which they feel resentful of any restrictions placed on them because of their sibling's condition. Remember that you can use some of the ideas discussed in Chapter 3 about children's understanding of illness for siblings as well, as their understanding of their brother or sister's illness will follow a similar progression through the developmental stages described in more detail in that chapter.

Witnessing Distress Due to Illness

Case Study – Sam (6 years old) and Jonny (8 years old)

Sam has asthma which has been getting worse and one night he has a severe asthma attack which does not seem to respond to the usual medication. His parents are both there and decide to call an ambulance. Just as the ambulance arrives, his older brother Jonny wakes up and, in a half-awake state, sees Sam, who is now panicking, being taken away in the ambulance with his mother.

Over the next few hours, his dad is in constant text contact with his mum, but it is confusing and hard to find out exactly what is going on. Jonny is sent back to bed but can't sleep and lies awake worrying.

Although Sam recovers well after this episode, Jonny remains anxious whenever he witnesses Sam getting breathless or when his asthma gets worse. He doesn't like being left with Sam for any length of time, as he fears he won't know what to do if something goes wrong.

Siblings of a child with a physical health condition can witness some very distressing episodes – for example, if their brother or sister is in pain or has to undergo difficult treatments because of their condition – and they will then need additional comfort and reassurance at these times. Their empathy with their brother or sister means they often feel pain or distress indirectly themselves and therefore do need to be comforted too. This can also be frightening for them, particularly if the situation feels 'out of control'; for example, if their parents also seem unsure what to do or are scared.

After a frightening event such as Sam and Jonny experienced, it can take a while to build up confidence again, and it is important to review any treatment plan with your child's medical team to understand what happened and to make sure the treatment plan is effective. If a sibling has witnessed the frightening event, but has not been part of the recovery (and the subsequent discussion about what happened and how the treatment plan should change), they can be left with uncertainties that need to be talked about and worked on, to help them build up confidence again. It is helpful to share the new treatment plan with a sibling, to show them what they should do if they are worried themselves, and also to give them a chance to talk about and understand what happened. It also reassures siblings to see that parents do have a plan and know what to do, and that siblings are not responsible for keeping their brother or sister safe.

Increased Independence

Studies show that brothers and sisters of children with a physical health condition often develop a higher level of maturity and independence compared to other children at the same developmental stage. For example, they may become involved in some caring tasks, even if it is something relatively minor, such as asking them to fetch something for you or to help distract a younger child by showing them a toy. They can quickly learn that they need to do more for themselves, such as help themselves to a drink, rather than waiting for you to get it for them. While there is a positive side to this increased independence, they do also need to have the opportunity to be a child, and their frustration and resentment may be expressed in various ways.

Case Study – Jenny (7 years old) and Kate (10 years old)

Jenny and Kate are sisters, and Kate has recently been diagnosed with Crohn's disease and has episodes of very bad stomach pains. Both girls are at a neighbour's house playing with friends when Kate starts to feel unwell. She is quite a shy girl who doesn't like to draw attention to herself but can't help occasionally putting her hand to her tummy when it hurts. Jenny notices this and, concerned for Kate, asks her friend's mum to call their mum because Kate is feeling unwell. Jenny is a bit upset but reassured when their mum comes to pick them up.

Some children react by becoming exceptionally 'good' and 'helpful', sensing the level of stress their parents are feeling and not wanting to upset them any further. This is a way of the sibling 'sharing' some of the care for the child and taking some responsibility themselves for managing the stress they can sense their parent is experiencing. This can result in them experiencing mixed or conflicting feelings – they feel upset or sad themselves, but they also want to make things better and cover up these feelings in order to either please other people or try and reduce the level of stress that they have realised others are feeling.

It can be helpful to give children permission to acknowledge these conflicting feelings and help them find a way of expressing them safely. First, aim to help them understand their emotions by labelling the feeling itself and by showing empathy for what they feel, then reflect this back to them to check if it is accurate. For example, 'It sounds to me like you are being brave about it, but part of you is feeling very sad because you can't do what you want to do. That's hard to be feeling like that – it's like you have mixed-up feelings.'

It can also be important to set up fun times when well children can be 'childish' and do something that is deliberately set up as free of responsibility. This is an example of a time when it can be helpful to use 'treats' to give them something which is enjoyable and focused on them. Sometimes relatives or friends can help with this, if it is hard to find the time yourself – it will also give them a break from 'caring', too. The Resources section at the back of this book includes some charities that support siblings and young carers, and which can signpost to additional support for siblings.

Genetic Conditions

In some families, more than one child may be affected by the same genetic medical condition. While the impact of the condition will vary for each individual child, there will be some commonalities, too. Although siblings may receive a similar type of daily treatment and therefore get a similar amount of parental attention, difficulties can still arise. A child may insist on a particular parent doing certain treatments, which can impact on flexibility. Siblings are very good at noticing when they aren't getting the same as each other and so sibling rivalry can occur in this situation, too. However, there are potential advantages for the siblings in that, as they get older, they might be a good emotional support for each other.

There may also be genetic 'carriers' in the family; for example, a parent who is not symptomatic of the condition, but who carries the genetic material that can be passed on to another child. Some of these conditions are X-chromosome linked, which means that while the mother is a carrier, only her sons will be affected, and daughters may or may not be carriers. Because our understanding of genetic conditions has advanced so much in recent years, the death of a child in a previous generation can be seen in a new light and understood to be due to the same condition as the child who is currently affected.

In some rare conditions, siblings can play a part in the treatment of their affected brother or sister; for example, if they are the best source of closely matched cells for a stem cell transplant, which is used to treat some types of cancer and other metabolic or immunodeficiency conditions. Given the ethical issues associated with asking a child to donate stem cells for the benefit of a sibling, this process is regulated by the Human Tissue Authority. It is considered good practice to ensure siblings have an age-appropriate understanding of the procedure and, where possible, to involve the sibling donor in the decision-making, even if they are not able to give consent themselves. Generally speaking, children have to be sixteen years of age to consent to a medical procedure, but it is possible for children younger than this to be competent to give consent if they have sufficient understanding of the risks and benefits of a procedure.

A stem cell transplant is still a high-risk medical procedure for the child having the transplant, so it is usually only offered if other treatment has not worked. Given the serious nature of the recipient's medical condition and the strong bonds between siblings, this can make the donor feel that they have no choice but to go ahead, so it is important for the donor to have the opportunity to understand (as best they can for their age) what the procedure involves for them, and to help prepare them for this.

Case Study – Alice (6 years old) and Claire (8 years old)

Alice has been treated for cancer but sadly this has recently relapsed, so she is now about to be admitted for a bone marrow transplant. Her older brother and sister have been tested to see if they are a 'match' for her to donate stem cells, and her older sister Claire has been found to be a good match. Alice's parents are delighted about this because they know that this gives Alice a much better chance of successful treatment but are also thinking about how hard this will be for all the family, because Alice will need to be in hospital for eight weeks having a demanding medical treatment.

They are also concerned about the procedure Claire will need to have to donate and how she feels about being the donor – Claire and Alice are close but, if anything, Alice is the more confident outgoing child, and Claire can be quite timid.

Claire has to come to hospital for a medical assessment to be a sibling donor, and the procedure is explained to her by the nursing team. She is given a copy of a book explaining the donation process called Jess Donates Bone Marrow *(published by the Children's Cancer and Leukaemia Group CCLG – see Resources section) and has a chance to look through this with her parents and ask questions about what will happen. She says she is happy to do this and clearly feels pleased to be 'chosen' to be a donor. But at the same time, she is also frightened of having a cannula put in as when she had her assessment she had a difficult experience having a blood test and becomes tearful thinking about this. Although she is still clear she wants to be the donor, she needs some help from a play specialist to help her manage the medical procedure itself. This support is arranged so that Claire has a plan for how to manage with the procedures needed before her operation and fortunately this helps it go more smoothly.*

Treats

Some parents comment that they themselves, and other people, overcompensate because they feel sorry for the sibling who is left out; for example, by buying them presents or taking them for treats. While some additional treats do help at times, there is also some value in trying to keep life as normal as possible for the sibling, rather than feeling that these treats are the only way to 'make up' for time when you aren't there. Parents often don't realise that the most powerful reward for their children is parental attention. Your well child will be more than happy having 'mum-time' or 'dad-time' sharing an activity together; it isn't necessary to buy expensive treats. One mother of a seven-year-old boy with a skin condition that requires a lot of daily treatment told us about her ten-year-old daughter who loves going with her in the car whenever she has an errand to run. She says, 'It isn't exciting, she just likes being in the car with me.'

Communication

It is important to remember to share information about the health condition with siblings, taking into account how much information they need to understand their sibling's condition. Sometimes, siblings say that they were never directly told about their brother or sister's condition and just picked up information from overhearing conversations. As they will not usually be included in medical appointments, they may not get information about any changes in treatment. If they are older than the unwell child, they may be able to take in and understand more than the unwell child or they may ask questions that are in advance of their sibling, which you may not be as prepared for. When at school or outside the home, they may be asked questions by other people about what is wrong with their brother and sister and need a way of being able to explain.

Sometimes, we think of the child with the medical condition when considering their developing understanding of their health and treatment requirements, but siblings need to be considered, too. The following conversation is an example of how a sibling may raise a concern about their brother or sister's illness, and how they may need an update from time to time about the condition or treatment. Nine-year-old Jaya has a seven-year-old brother, Dylan, who has cystic fibrosis:

Jaya: *Mum, some girls in my class said that Dylan is a drug addict . . . he takes drugs all the time.*

Mum: *What did you say?*

Jaya: *I said he isn't a drug addict, leave him alone. You don't know what you're talking about. But then I just ran away and I felt really sad. I cried a bit but no one saw me.*

Mum: *I don't want you to ever feel sad at school because of what some of the children say. You are a good*

> *girl for telling me about it. Would it be helpful if*
> *you had something ready prepared to say if these*
> *girls or anyone else says something about Dylan*
> *again?*

Jaya: *Yes, it would be good . . . what can I say?*

Mum: *Well, if anyone asks Dylan why he is taking tab-*
lets, he just says, 'It helps me digest my food,'
and that seems to do the trick. Would you like to
say the same?

Jaya: *Thank you, Mum, I'll say that, too. Is that really*
why Dylan takes tablets? Will you tell me about
it?

Jaya was prompted by an incident at school to ask for more information about her brother's medical condition. Sometimes it does come out of the blue like this. Parents often find it is better to give information when it is needed, rather than explaining everything all at once.

It is important to give siblings the chance to update their understanding of their brother or sister's condition by checking if they have questions they want to ask. Some charities or hospitals run family days which can include siblings, and where they can meet other siblings in a simi- lar position to themselves. This can be a really valuable way of helping children feel less isolated, as well as being a fun and informative day.

Case Study – Muhammed (7 years old) and Isha (9 years old)

Muhammed is seven and has been diagnosed with a rare kidney cancer, which involves a lot of treatment in hospital and he is currently out of school. His older sister Isha is nine and has been feeling a bit tearful and upset at times.

One day at school she bursts into tears after a minor falling out with her friend and tells her teacher a bit about what is happening at home. At the end of the day, her teacher asks to meet Isha's father who is picking her up to discuss how best to help Isha. Her father is a bit reluctant but agrees for Isha to join a group the school runs one lunchtime a week for eight weeks specifically for children who need emotional support. The group involves craft activities but is also facilitated by a therapist from the local Emotional Wellbeing services who includes some activities to help children talk about emotions and problem-solve together. Isha enjoys the group and feels more confident to talk about her concerns.

It is usually helpful to tell the nursery or school for both your unwell child and their sibling a bit about what they are experiencing at home, so that they can understand if they show any signs of upset at school. Normal routines like school become even more important for children when there are disruptions at home, and can really help by being a time when the child is living a 'normal' life in the same way as other children of their age.

They may also be able to access some additional support via school, and the advantage of this is that it can be done in a non-stigmatising way since it takes place as part of the normal school day. One example of this is the work done by the charity 'Place2Be' which provides counselling within the school environment, on both an individual or group basis (see Resources at the end of the book).

Sibling Rivalry

Siblings often have very intense relationships – they have so much in common, sharing both some of their physical characteristics and the family environment with each other. While brothers and sisters can be very close, there is usually an element of competition and rivalry between them, and these conflicting feelings of caring for – but also resenting – their brother or sister often give rise to a sense of guilt which, in itself, can be very distressing. The intensity of these feelings can be overwhelming and, as we all know, sibling rivalry often continues into adulthood as well. It can be very hard for a child to admit to these feelings in the face of everyone else showing high levels of concern and compassion towards the unwell child.

As a parent, it can be helpful if you can accept this rivalry and show them you can tolerate these strong feelings, first by modelling a calm response, and second by showing them that there are safe ways to express such anger. Much of the usual squabbling that goes on between siblings can be safely ignored. Most of the time, it is better to ignore it than to respond, even if you do find it irritating. Children generally find attention rewarding and this includes the attention they receive when you tell them off; ignoring squabbling ensures that you are not unintentionally rewarding this behaviour by giving it your attention. This can be particularly difficult to do if you are upset or tired, or if this is a sensitive area for you (e.g., if your sibling used to do the same thing to you).

When you are feeling stressed, it is hard to hold on to the empathy for your child's feelings. We all reach that point occasionally, so it is important for us as the adult to take notice of this and identify what it is that we ourselves need in order to try to manage the situation better. For example, you may recognise that you are not being consistent with a sibling because you feel sorry for them as they are missing out (see Chapter 5 on managing behaviour), whereas actually what they need you to do is to continue with some consistent rules or boundaries.

Case Study – Sarah (4 years old) and Emma (10 years old)

Sarah has serious food allergies and has recently had to go on a 'few foods' diet to try and establish which foods are safe for her and which are causing the problems. She has an older brother Callum, aged seven, with no food issues, but her ten-year-old sister Emma has always been a fussy eater and has only ever reluctantly eaten family meals, preferring to snack in between.

Emma now starts insisting that she wants to choose her own food as well and that it is not fair that she has to eat what she doesn't like and will only eat the foods she likes. Her mother is already finding it difficult to manage Sarah's diet, and she has been struggling to give Emma the attention she normally does, so she reluctantly goes along with Emma's requests to try and avoid arguing with her at mealtimes, and increasingly ends up preparing three separate meals – one for Sarah, one for Emma and one for the rest of the family.

This comes to a head one afternoon when Emma changes her mind about the meal she wants, and refuses to eat what she had chosen earlier. Her mother realises she needs to be firm and clear with Emma and decides not to offer her another choice. Emma refuses to eat the meal, which is hard for her mother to tolerate, but it is worth it because Emma realises this isn't a good strategy to get her own way. Her mother then works towards a compromise, so Emma can have something that she has chosen, but also has to have some of the family meal.

Building Co-operation between Siblings

It can help to try and find some positive tasks that siblings can do together or to give them some joint tasks to do to help build alliances where they might actually find out that they can do something more easily when they co-operate. Sometimes, achieving the task more easily is rewarding in itself and so they don't actually need a reward as such afterwards.

The following ideas can be helpful to build co-operation between siblings.

Taking turns

Introduce the idea of taking turns as well as sharing and help them to hand over willingly at the end of their turn.

Some children are very good at finding ways to avoid 'handing over' at the end of their turn, so you do need to be prepared to step in to make it happen.

Solve it yourselves

Try not to take sides by not responding to a child coming to 'tell tales' on the others. Otherwise, they will learn that they can find a way of building an alliance with you which effectively 'splits' the sibling group. Instead, encourage them to take some responsibility for finding a way to resolve a dispute. Encourage them to do some of the problem-solving – naming what the problem is and getting them to think of possible ways of resolving it; for example, when they are fighting over a toy/game get them to decide what the rule should be about who gets it first – if they can't find a solution then neither of them gets it, whereas if they can, then they can take turns having it.

Family rules

Develop some family rules that are applied to all consistently – choose from the factors that are most important to you as a family, because after a while these will become part of the fabric of family life. This will be useful when your child realises that not all families have the same rules and compares their lot with other families: e.g., 'In our family we don't hurt people either by hitting them or by teasing them' or 'We always respect each other.'

Different is OK

Make valuing difference a core family value – this helps with competition and therefore with rivalry. Never compare siblings with each other and instead talk positively about any special differences.

Key Points

- You can't be a perfect parent to all your children all the time; aim to be 'good enough'.

- Make the most of others who can substitute for you, such as family or friends.

- Help your well children understand any routine hospital or doctor appointment and show them how you are going to manage these. Update them with key information about their siblings' health needs, as and when it comes up.

- Find a 'special time' for you to spend time together – short is OK as long as it is reliable – use technology to help with this.

- Plan 'fun' times for them so they can still enjoy being a child.

- Find ways to build co-operation between siblings.

- Limits still need to be set!

10

Adolescence and Managing Transition to Adulthood and Adult Health Services

Adolescence is the stage of development between childhood and adulthood and, for most adults, especially parents, talking about this stage is often accompanied by a groan. The end stage of childhood and the transition to becoming an adult is marked by particular behaviours that almost all teenagers display to some extent or another. It is worthwhile considering what happens during this phase of life that may result in some challenging behaviours for all parents; and, for parents of teenagers with a physical health condition, possibly more so.

In general, the adolescent phase, which is now accepted to be between ten years and about twenty-five years of age, is the healthiest period of the lifespan. During this stage, physical development results in increases in strength, speed, reaction time and immune function, and improved resistance to physical stressors such as cold, heat, hunger and dehydration. Yet, this phase is also marked by an increase in rates of serious injury. So, from the time that parents start to lose some control over their offspring, they hit a worrying period. This is particularly concerning for parents of teenagers who also need to manage treatments or other aspects of their health. This chapter helps parents encourage independence in their teenagers while making sure health is managed well.

There is often an increase in risk-taking, sensation-seeking and erratic behaviour during adolescence. Most teenagers will present some or all of these typical behaviours, but there is still a lot of variation between individuals. Young people with physical illness go through this developmental phase just like everyone else. There may be several illness-related and physiological causes for changes in physical health, but it may also be that behaviours and attitudes typical of this developmental phase are also contributory factors.

Brain Changes during Adolescence

Using the more sophisticated scanning technology that is now available, in the last few years it has been possible to study the changes in the developing adolescent brain and to measure how these impact on behaviour. The major changes in the adolescent brain result in improvements in intelligence and behaviour such that your child starts to be able to act like an adult. These changes include:

- Development of critical thinking and decision-making

- Ability to process information faster

- Development of skills improving thinking ahead and planning (executive functioning)

- Increased ability to control behaviour by thinking before acting

All of these mean this is the start of your child being capable of looking after themselves, being able to speak for themselves in medical appointments and knowing how to manage their treatments and stay well. After all, your child knows how they are feeling better than you do and so encouraging and teaching them to manage their own health will result in better overall management.

However, the brain takes some time to achieve these end results and, during adolescence, we usually see some increased capabilities, but also some behaviour such as mood swings or acting before thinking, reflecting less mature development. Over many years, the brain undergoes a period of restructuring in order to become more efficient, quicker at thinking, better at organising, storing and ordering information, sorting what is important from what is trivial, decision-making and planning. The young person's body also grows rapidly in this phase, with vast hormonal changes that determine the rate of this development on an individual basis. There are great variations in the timing and rate of physiological, pubertal and neurological changes among children and adolescents and this in itself can pose problems for some individuals – changing too soon or too late in comparison to peers can be difficult.

While the brain and body are 'under construction', we see some behaviour that results in tensions between the adolescent and their parents or other adults. For example, adolescents may believe that they are able to go out independently but will not have thought ahead to remember to take their bus pass. They still need someone to look out for them, but will protest if you check them and accuse you of nagging.

During this 'transitional' time, many of the following behaviours are common:

- Difficulty in interpreting the emotions of others

- Difficulty in regulating their own emotions

- Rapid mood changes that do not seem to be warranted

- Extremes of mood – your teenager won't just be sad, they will be severely miserable; they won't just be happy, they will be triumphant

- An increase in reckless behaviour – acting without thinking through the consequences first

- Difficulty in considering the long-term consequences of their behaviour because they cannot yet put all the facts together to reason it through

All of the above are perfectly normal when related to the underlying changes that are occurring in the brain. For more detail of these changes in adolescence, it may be helpful to see the TED talk by Sarah-Jayne Blakemore (reference in the Resources section).

For parents of teenagers with a physical health condition, some of the risks your adolescent may take may include those that affect the management of their illness, which could potentially have a significant effect on the young person's health outcome in the long term. Supporting your child from childhood to adulthood is difficult enough, but when you have to negotiate handing over managing treatments to your teenager, it introduces an additional set of worries.

Responsibility and Decision-making around Treatment

As your child gets older, they will gradually become more involved in decision-making and will have more responsibility over their treatment decisions. At some point, your child's healthcare teams may recommend to you that you start to hand over managing treatments because this is now 'age-appropriate'. While you know that at some point you need to do this, you also know your own teenager better than anyone else and, although they may look like an adult, you may feel that mentally and emotionally they are not ready to manage their treatment independently.

From fairly early on in their childhood, it is important to make a note to yourself that one day they will have responsibility for looking after themselves. It might be useful to bear in mind that you have a few years to be able to 'train them up'. As with all transitions, this is a process rather than a one-off event, so it is best to start the process gradually and accept it may take a while to achieve before your teenager can take over full responsibility.

One of the biggest fears that parents of teenagers with medical needs have is that their child won't manage their care to the same standards that you have achieved up to this point. You know how much time, effort and worry has gone into keeping them well. For this reason, you may feel you can't yet bring yourself to hand over full responsibility to your fifteen-year-old son or daughter. You may already have bad memories of previous occasions when they made errors or were not able to assess how ill they were.

But it is important to remember that sticking to a treatment regime can be a problem at any age, and people with long-term health conditions (and even those of us without!) often make choices not to follow a prescribed treatment plan, or to change the plan, without informing the doctor or prescriber. These choices can be based on many different factors, such as:

- Considering our own judgement about the necessity of the treatment to be better than that of the person who prescribed it

- A lack of understanding of how the medicine should be taken

- Poor quality of information or explanation from the healthcare team

- The impact of the medicine or whole treatment package on daily life – for example, it may be too time-consuming, conspicuous or complex

It is worth considering whether any of the above reasons are relevant, so that you can address the underlying reason for your adolescent's choice, if necessary.

Handing over Treatment Responsibilities

To begin handing over responsibility for treatment to your child, it is worth starting the process with something they are most likely to find easy to achieve and gradually work up to them taking full responsibility. It can be helpful to think of this as a gradual or phased approach.

Phase 1 – Steps to Teach Your Child to Manage Their Own Treatment

1. Choose an easy medicine or treatment that you know your child can already manage, e.g., swallowing a tablet.

2. Tell your child that you have noticed that they do it well and so you don't have to be responsible for that medicine these days.

3. Tell your child that they can be given responsibility for it. You will check in case it is forgotten.

4. Initially be available to remind them if necessary.

5. Once they routinely and reliably take the medicine, leave it to them.

6. Occasionally say that it is great they can look after that medicine.

7. Think of any other aspects of their treatment regimen they could now take responsibility for.

The most successful way to implement this is to start before your child becomes a teenager, when you as a parent are more influential and they are less focused on other factors, such as what their friends think and fitting in with their peers.

Understanding Adolescent Motivation

Returning to the maturing brain, we now understand that one of the aims of brain restructuring is to develop skills in organising, planning and being able to forward-think to get things ready (called 'executive skills'). As an adult and a parent, you will be familiar with all the tasks you need to put in place in order to get everyone ready for school and work in the morning. Now consider how much of that you think your teenager can do. They are likely to be capable of some but not all of the planning and preparation needed

– and, of course, this varies according to individual rates of development. As an adult, you are capable of planning, thinking ahead and assessing the requirements of tasks and the time needed to succeed, and can then 'think backwards' about when to begin.

You are motivated to do this because you can see the benefits of the outcome you are working towards (e.g., not being late for work) and can plan your behaviour to avoid the pitfalls. Teenagers aren't able to do this yet because their motivations are different from yours. Their stage of brain development means they are more focused on immediate reward (such as extra time in bed) and less concerned with taking risks (getting into trouble or missing treatments).

Some of the rewards for an adolescent with a physical health condition are likely to include:

- Being the same as their friends – a strong desire for peer identification

- Excitement from exploratory (risky) behaviour – smoking, alcohol use, not doing treatment

- Relationships with friends and emotional separation from parents

- Exploring their identity and trying out different behaviours – who am I and what will I become?

Challenges for the Adolescent with a Physical Health Condition

As a result of your child's illness, they may need to attend clinics, have regular treatments that may be complex and conspicuous and sometimes may need to be admitted to hospital. They may have a reduced physical capacity compared to their peers and be reliant on parents and healthcare professionals. All this comes at a stage of life when they are more motivated to seek out rewards and to avoid anything that gets in the way of this, alongside a strong need to be like their friends. This may result in challenges in many areas, including:

• Not being able to be as autonomous as they would like

• Personal identity – are they a normal person who is sick or a sick person trying to be normal?

• Social maturity – has the impact of the condition reduced their ability to socialise and have friendships?

• Sexuality and relationships – are these affected by the illness?

• Educational and vocational choices – has the illness or missed school meant that they haven't realised their potential?

Support for the Teenager with a Physical Health Condition

You need support and education, too! Most healthcare teams will offer support to parents about managing the teenage years and, specifically, how to begin to hand over control to their child for managing the condition and treatment. Because of the risk that your teenager will not manage their own health as well as you have done, you may need reassurance and guidance over how to begin this process. This is part of understanding the changes in your relationship with your child as you move from the parent of a child to the parent of an emerging adult.

Although earlier in this chapter (in Phase 1), we discussed some strategies for encouraging responsibility for simple medical tasks, sometimes teenagers are reluctant or unwilling to take responsibility for their treatment. The following is a very typical exchange between parent and teenager in most families. In this example, the teenager, Nick, is fifteen years old:

> Mum: *Nick, come in here and do your [nebuliser/inhaler/injection/physio . . . any required treatment].*
>
> Nick: *[Silence, no response.]*
>
> Mum: *Nick, I said come and do your [treatment].*
>
> Nick: *[Mumbles.]*

Mum: NICK!!!!

Nick: GET OFF MY CASE . . . SHUT UP . . . LEAVE
           ME ALONE. I'LL DO IT WHEN I'M READY!!!!

Mum: [Silence.]

This scenario may be repeated in similar ways – it might have several more rounds of mum shouting before she gets an abusive response from her teenager – but it ends in a very unsatisfactory way on both sides. And yet, it may also be repeated day in and day out. What happens is this:

1. Mum sees the time is ready for her son to do his treatment, so she calls out to him. Nick is busy communicating with his friends in his bedroom on his laptop, so his mum shouting feels like an attack: 'Turn off the computer and do your treatment . . .' Nick feels punished.

2. In response to feeling attacked by mum, who is preventing him from continuing his rewarding activity of speaking to friends, he ignores her.

3. Any behaviour that is ignored always results initially in us trying again. Mum applies her 'attack' once again, and shouts louder.

4. Nick chooses this time not to avoid but to attack; he shouts back, louder and abusively: 'Stop going on . . . you are always getting at me . . . I will do it LATER!!!!!' His mother feels punished herself, and either attacks back with increased anger or walks away.

5. Mum will either continue in rounds of further shouting or will retreat. Mum removing her instruction to do the treatment has worked for Nick, as he gets to continue speaking to his friends.

6. Mum has inadvertently taught Nick that when she calls for him to do his treatment, if he shouts enough at her, then she will not make him do it. This sequence of events is a trap that it is very easy to fall into, and all parents do it at times.

How to Encourage Responsibility in Your Teenager

Once you know that your teenager is aware of everything they need to know about the treatments they require, what you as parents want from them is to be able to trust that they will look after themselves well. The following gives some ideas about how to encourage trustworthiness in regard to looking after their own health and managing treatment requirements:

Phase 2 – Steps to Encourage Trustworthy Independence

1. **Reward** – teenagers like rewards! One of the most valuable rewards of this stage is some *freedom*. A sleepover, going to the shopping mall/hanging out with friends, going away for the weekend, going to a festival.

2. **Rules** – there is no way you are going to allow this level of freedom without you knowing you can trust your teenager to take some *responsibility*. So you set clear rules, set up some training and tests: 'If you can show me for the next week that you can take your injections, then I will consider letting you go.'

3. **Risk** – you as parents take the risk first. Once you have set up clear rules and training, you let them have a go. But you are ready with your *back-up plan*. You will have thought in advance of everything that could go wrong and have in mind what will have to happen if this is the case.

4. **Rescue** – it is not the end of the world if your teenager needs some extra input managing their condition after they have had their freedom. Rather than taking back control, just *renegotiate* your rules for next time (e.g., 'Next time you have a sleepover you need to bring forward the time of your injection, so do it before you go and I know it has been done.')

The Role of the Healthcare Team and Transition from Paediatric to Adult Healthcare Services

By the time your teenager has reached seventeen years of age, it is important that the healthcare team help you and your teenager in managing the transition from childhood to adulthood and also from a paediatric health centre to an adult health centre. It may be that your teenager has good relationships with the adult healthcare team already but, if not, it is worth suggesting that they find the time to have a talk with one of the team at a routine appointment on their own. Of course, adolescents are notoriously private, and they don't like to disclose their innermost thoughts, especially to adults who are relatively unknown to them. But if they aren't offered this opportunity, they are unlikely to request it themselves.

This includes always ensuring confidentiality. This may be of concern to you, but remember, this is in the context of enabling your teenager to become a responsible adult managing their own healthcare. Importantly, if healthcare professionals have concerns that someone is at risk or is being harmed, they must then break confidentiality in the interests of the child. In reality, this isn't usually necessary because the healthcare professionals will try and work with your teenager to find mutually agreed ways of being able to include you in anything they think you should know, even if no risk is involved.

In the same way that transferring responsibility for healthcare management from you to your teenager strikes you with fear and trepidation, many parents feel the same about moving care from a well-trusted paediatric healthcare team to a new adult healthcare team, quite possibly in a different hospital or location. Paediatric centres should now all have transition policies and practices, and it has been a goal for the NHS to require paediatric centres to achieve set transition standards. The detail of the transition policy and practice may vary depending on location and on the medical condition.

The first requirement for transition to occur, not surprisingly, is the existence of good, adequately resourced services in an adult healthcare setting. The second requirement is that transition is accepted as a process, not a single event. Transition should begin several years before the age (usually sixteen or seventeen years) at which a person has care transferred from one centre to another. There must be time for the young person, their family and the new healthcare team to get to know each other. Again, this will vary depending on the type of medical condition and health needs.

Some long-term conditions have well established packages of care which are mostly delivered and reviewed in an outpatient clinic. Some conditions will be more unpredictable than others, and the decision to transfer care may be based on the stage of the illness or the resources available at an adult centre. However, in general, the most appropriate care for an adult is within an adult centre, as paediatric centres do not normally have the experience or knowledge – or sometimes even the resources required – for medical investigations or surgery to manage medical conditions in an adult patient. They are therefore often unable to offer emotional support or deal effectively with adult lifestyle concerns.

There are some agreed aspects of transition that most paediatric healthcare teams follow in collaboration with the adult services transitioned to, and these are often referred to as 'standards':

1. Transition must be a collaboration between paediatric and adult centres. You and your child need to know that the paediatric team know the adult team and share the same standards in the delivery of care.

2. Psychological and practical preparation should be provided from the paediatric team well in advance of the moment of transfer of care. Most paediatric centres recommend that discussions about eventual transition start at about thirteen or fourteen years of age.

3. It is important to begin preparing your child early on to be more independent so that they can cope when they transfer to an adult centre. This will mean supporting your child to understand their medical condition and treatment needs. It might also include knowing how to monitor drugs at home and how to re-order them from the pharmacy. This is not because you will disappear, but, while you are there as a 'safety net', you can pass on your skills and knowledge.

4. Your teenager will need practice at being able to speak up for themselves in medical consultations. Even if they still need some support to do so, it is important that they are treated as the central, most important person in the consultation. For some teenagers, this might mean attending the whole or part of the consultation alone.

5.   The paediatric team must be careful not to show a bias for one adult centre over another (if there is a choice). They must respect the rights of the teenager, offer guidance and support, discuss the future, provide information about the adult services, and facilitate the move both practically and emotionally.

6.   At the most basic level, you and your teenager should expect to receive an information pack from the paediatric centre which will also include information on adult services if there are some that are well known to the paediatric team; attend joint paediatric and adult clinics which are normally held in the paediatric centre with a team from the adult service attending and seeing the teenagers alongside their paediatric colleagues; make informal visits to the adult centres and the adult team should be available for you and your child to speak to prior to the actual transfer of care.

7.   The process includes:

   *   Raising the issue of transition early

   *   A flexible approach to age of transfer

   *   Promoting some independence in the young person – for example, being seen alone at the start of the appointment by the healthcare professional

   *   Discussion and planning with the young person and family

   *   Liaison between paediatric and adult team members

*   No further contact with the paediatric centre after the final transfer

8.   Finally, transition should become a normal, expected practice.

Key Points

- Adolescence is a time of great change physically and mentally and it is common for young people to take more risks during this phase of development.

- Adolescents may not fully accept the consequences of the importance of sticking to a treatment regime to prevent future illness or complications – they may either not be motivated to do so, or may not consider the risks in the same way an adult would.

- They will be more likely to ask 'What would my friends do?' rather than 'What would my parents/doctor/nurse do?'

- Handing over responsibility to your adolescent should take place over several years and is a gradual process.

- Encourage your adolescent to see a member of the healthcare team on their own.

- This can be an anxious time for parents, so you may also need support in managing this.

- The transition process from child services to adult services should start well before their care is transferred.

11

Caring for Yourself and Your Relationships

If you are lucky, you may have a strong support structure around you that includes family, friends and local resources such as parent groups, as well as the more formal health support systems such as your health visitor and GP. Good family and social support can be invaluable and, for many people, it is close friends, grandparents, aunts, uncles and other family members who provide most of the practical and emotional support you need when you have a child with a long-term illness. Not everyone is lucky enough to have this sort of support, and even when it is in place, difficulties can arise at times of increased stress or crisis, and relationships can become strained. Resentment can easily build up and this gets in the way of clear communication, which can contribute to difficulties and lead to more resentment.

Some parents who take on a caring role for a child with a long-term illness also say that they feel they have lost their previous identity as an adult. For example, they may have had strong positive relationships at work with colleagues and their sense of self-esteem may have come from achievements in the workplace. When you have a child with a medical condition, it can be hard to keep up the same links with work in the short term after diagnosis, and in the longer term it can mean changing expectations and priorities. It can feel like you have been thrown into a world you are much less comfortable with, and one which doesn't allow you to have the control you are used to. This can be a very difficult transition and can make parents feel that they have lost their own sense of confidence or self-value. While many employers will be sympathetic and do give time off work to care for a child, it is still difficult to have the flexibility to take time off for unexpected illnesses or hospital admissions.

Over time, families develop their own rules of what works for them and build up their own family routines and structure. However, there are many ways of doing this, and no short cut to finding what works for your family. There will inevitably be times when it is a real struggle and when the juggling feels overwhelming, particularly if a parent needs some flexibility to take time off if the child is ill or in hospital.

Many parents of babies with long-term illnesses say they feel very isolated from the 'normal' support strategies that new parents usually use in these situations – even other members of the family can be very shocked, frightened or even judgemental about a child with health needs. While other new parents are preoccupied with their own child and 'normal' challenges, such as getting sleep and feeding patterns established, this may seem trivial compared to the challenges faced by a parent with a child with a health condition. In addition, other new parents may not have the emotional space or capacity to take someone else's additional needs into account.

If you are on your own or have limited support from your own family, or have a family in conflict, this can be a very isolating experience. It can be hard to find the additional confidence and energy to get involved in activities outside the home, and all of these may need you to be highly organised. It may help to bring a friend or relative to appointments with you when you can. It can be helpful to talk through any decisions you have to make about your child's healthcare; often it is hard to remember everything that was said on the day of the appointment, so having someone else there can help you remember details.

Identifying a good friend who can get to understand a bit about your child's illness and even help with some aspects of treatment or give you a break occasionally can be really helpful.

Practical Support

We know that there are increased financial burdens on families with a child with a long-term illness. Even if healthcare itself is free at the point of delivery, all the additional costs such as fares to get to and from hospital, parking at the hospital or taking time off from work to bring a child to appointments can add up. Parents may have taken the decision for one parent to give up working or work part-time or flexible hours in order to be around for the medical demands required. Financial and practical strains can build up and lead to emotional stress as well.

There are some sources of financial support that families with a child with a long-term illness might be eligible for, depending on your child's level of need and your level of income. However, it is not always straightforward to find out what you are entitled to. In some hospitals there are family support workers or social work services that can offer this support, and some charities also fund some additional support (for example, CLIC Sargent fund social workers who offer practical and emotional support to all families where a child is diagnosed with cancer). If you are not sure if you are eligible for any financial support, then the Citizens Advice Bureau can offer advice and guidance about sources of support (see Resources section at the end of the book).

For many parents, there are practical issues that get in the way of the help they need. Ideally, they would like to have a break, but it is difficult to find reliable carers who are able to provide the sort of care required. While some services are available from social care funded by your local author-ity, these are frequently extremely limited and involve assessments that can be time-consuming so will not solve the problem immediately.

Some people are very wary about accepting a referral to social care, and fear that their child might be taken away from them or that they will be judged as inadequate as a parent. However, these services are there to provide sup-port for families, although they are often not able to provide as much support as would be ideal. They are essential if a child needs a package of care at home and, depending on the area you live in, some are able to provide short breaks or small amounts of support time at home.

There are also many charities that are linked to a particu-lar medical condition or diagnosis; some of them are very well-known, such as Macmillan Cancer Support, but there are also some for rare conditions that have been set up by an interested parent or relative. These are usually easy to find on the Internet, but if not then 'Contact a Family' has an online searchable list which can help locate the appro-priate service (see the Resources section).

Charities for specific medical conditions are often very

well informed about whether there is any financial support that families can access and can signpost families to them. Some provide access to additional resources to support carers (for example the CarersUK advice line).

Patient support groups and charities can also put people in touch with other parents who have been in a similar position, which can be a very powerful source of support because other parents really do have a good understanding of your child's condition and the specific challenges you face. For very rare conditions, it can help to find someone, possibly even in a different country, whose child has a similar diagnosis or experience to your own, since this may be very hard or impossible to find in your local area. These additional sources of information and support are also listed in the Resources section of this book.

While the Internet and social network sites provide a potentially strong link to other people in a similar position, it is important to be careful when using online chat rooms or social media – the information may not always be accurate, and every child is different, so what another parent experiences may be very different from your own experience. While social media can be a very valuable source of support, it can also give you access to very frightening information that it is then almost impossible to ignore!

Hospices are usually associated in most people's minds with end-of-life care, and many parents are understandably a bit fearful of what these services might be like.

However, hospices do actually provide a range of services for children and have a broad definition of what is meant by 'palliative care'. This includes children with a life-limiting condition who are nonetheless well at present but may have a reduced life expectancy. They are usually financed by charities and so have limited resources, but many provide excellent care for the whole family including parents, grandparents and siblings, and can link in with hospital services to complement the support offered within mainstream healthcare.

Looking After Yourself

When you are looking after children, especially children with health problems, it can be hard to look after yourself as well. Looking after yourself includes all the basic essentials such as making sure you are eating OK, sleeping enough and taking care of your own health. Parenting is a long-term project and keeping yourself well will help you manage the short-term difficulties that you face.

As we have seen throughout the book, it is also essential to consider your own psychological wellbeing alongside the wellbeing of your child. As we've discussed, how your child copes will be affected by how you cope and so, if you are feeling very stressed, this is likely to be picked up by your child. At times, when you do find it overwhelming, it is important to try and manage this, not just for your own sake, but in order to help your child as well. Rather than feeling you have to admit you are not coping, try to see this as normal and to be expected for a parent who has to manage more than the average parent!

There are no easy answers to finding the time and energy to look after yourself as well as your child, and it may only be realistic to do much less than you know is ideal. Nonetheless, it is easy to let your own needs slip to the bottom of the pile of things to do, so try and build in small amounts of time where you do something that makes you feel better.

What Other Parents Have Found Helpful

There are small things that you can do to help you feel better in the short term, which can help sustain you and help you feel more positive.

Treat yourself

Find something you can 'treat' yourself to. It is easy to be dismissive of even small tokens but this may realistically be all that is achievable at busy times and can help you to break out of a rut. Feeling resigned to the fact that very little can help can be a sign of feeling depressed, and this can itself prevent you from getting the help you need. Examples other parents have suggested include:

- Have a pamper session in the bath

- Do something creative, such as painting or colouring, writing a story or poem or icing a cake

- Set a timer for fifteen minutes and make it your time – do nothing or read a magazine – your choice!

- Change is as good as a rest – bring some flowers into the house, wear something bright, do something different

- Make a list of things you are grateful for or which are going well

- Listen to some music or sing – whatever you enjoy

Take a break

Getting some exercise and being outdoors has also recently become recognised as part of a helpful approach to managing stress or low mood. The natural reaction to feeling low is often to withdraw from your usual activities – it feels too much like hard work to get yourself out of the house, or you may feel bad about the way you look or ashamed of appearing tearful. It is also very common to withdraw from social contacts, maybe feeling you are too boring or feeling inadequate compared to other parents. But withdrawing is actually very bad for your mood – it means you spend more time 'in your head' brooding about how difficult things are or worrying about things. Whenever possible, take a break by doing something active; for example, going for a short walk, and include some contact with other people if possible.

Dealing with stressful thoughts

Mindfulness is an approach to managing stress that has become very popular in recent years. There is now a range of books and apps that introduce you to the principles of mindfulness. While it may be difficult to find the time to attend a weekly course of mindfulness sessions, it is something that can be done at home, by yourself, at your own pace. Some people find mindfulness-based stress reduction helpful for the management of stress. You may be able to access a free course via your GP but, if not, there is a variety of apps on the market, some of which are listed at the end of the book in the Resources section.

Many people feel uncomfortable with the early stages of mindfulness – it may feel embarrassing, or you feel self-conscious and find the 'hippy' approach unnatural. It is not for everyone but, because of its accessibility via phone apps and new technology, it has been taken up by many more people and become very popular. It has largely replaced stress management courses and there is now good evidence that it does help with managing stress.

Don't be too hard on yourself

Everyone has bad days, and sometimes it can be helpful to accept you have to write off today and start again tomorrow.

When Should I Get Help?

It can be hard to admit to yourself when you are finding it hard to cope. You may feel hopeless, that you are not doing a good enough job as a parent, or that there is nothing that can help make things better for you. Although there won't be any easy outright solutions, it is important for the longer term to seek help when you need it. There is still a lot of stigma associated with mental health problems, and it is also hard to find time to address these difficulties alongside all the other physical difficulties that you face.

There are services that may be able to help – your GP or your local hospital should have ways of referring you to a psychologist or a counsellor, and your local mental health services should be able to offer an assessment. You can also refer yourself to your local IAPT service, and there is information about how to do this in the Resources section. (IAPT stands for 'Improving Access to Psychological Therapy' and is an NHS initiative to improve the availability of talking therapy).

Case Study – Sara

Sara was an experienced teacher who had worked for several years as a head of department in a secondary school. She enjoyed her job and felt valued and confident about her skills. However, her baby arrived early at thirty-two weeks and she felt completely unprepared for this.

For the first few weeks he was in a special care baby unit and, although she spent most of the time by his side taking care of him, she felt clumsy and incompetent compared to the nurses. She had intended to breastfeed but struggled to get feeding established using a breast pump. Because of all the anxiety about her baby's low weight, she felt under pressure to provide breast milk for her son. When he was discharged home three weeks later, her partner had already returned to work after paternity leave, and she found it hard to get out of the house because of trying to set up a routine for her baby and trying to make sure he fed enough to grow. She had joined an antenatal group for new mothers in her area and gradually all the other mothers had their babies. They appeared so much healthier and stronger than her baby, so she felt 'left out' by the group because they all appeared to be managing so much better than her.

On a visit to her GP, when asked how she was getting on, she burst into tears. Her GP was sympathetic and reassuring and talked to her about how to get more help. She assessed Sara for postnatal depression and talked to her about support for new mothers. Sara was referred to her local mental health service by her GP and was seen for a series of six sessions based on cognitive behaviour therapy (CBT) to help manage her depression. Although Sara still struggled with the early months, she gradually built up her confidence and established good relationships with other local mothers.

Your Relationships

It is all too easy to put your own needs and relationship with your partner to the bottom of the pile when you are caring for a child with a physical condition. You may simply not have the time and energy to think about how to focus on your partner's needs, but nurturing your relationship will give it a better chance of surviving.

A lot will depend on where you start from when you realise you have a child with a long-term health problem. Some couples start from a really solid foundation and are very secure in their relationship with each other and may also be financially and socially well supported too. At the other end of the spectrum, your relationship may already be in difficulty, and you may find that the additional stresses of caring for a child mean that the relationship does break down. Couples who work well together are generally able to communicate well and value each other's contribution to the relationship. It is too easy to start feeling critical about what your partner does (or doesn't) do, but remember there are several different ways to approach and solve a problem, not just one way, so take time to listen to each other's points of view.

Whether you are out all day working, or at home caring for children, you may both find your day hard, and then find it hard to get the support you need from each other. If you are the parent who takes the lead in taking your child to outpatient appointments and giving them the treatment they need, you may find it hard to allow your partner to take over care because they do it less well than you. Your child may also begin to prefer that you do all the care. This, of course, makes it harder for your partner to become competent, as they don't get as much practice and don't have the same confidence when dealing with treatment.

Working together as a team can help share the burden of care but there are lots of obstacles that can get in the way of this. It can be hard to communicate your needs without resentment building up, and it can be hard to find any time just to enjoy being together. But not paying some attention to your relationship is likely to result in a build-up of frustration and communication difficulties.

Case Study – Ben (13 months old)

Sue and Tom have two children, Joshua aged three and Ben aged thirteen months, who has been diagnosed with eczema and severe food allergies. Tom works full-time and Sue worked part-time after Joshua was born and is now due to return to work from maternity leave.

Ben is very unsettled at night because of his eczema and is a very clingy baby. He has become very used to his mum holding him a lot of the time and so, when both parents are together, Tom tends to spend time with Joshua and Sue with Ben.

Sue has been looking into childcare and has found that the nursery that Joshua has been attending is not happy to accept responsibility for managing the safety and risk issues because of Ben's allergies. Sue used to enjoy her job and wants to return to work but does not feel Ben is happy when left with others. She and Tom are constantly tired and sleep-interrupted and have been arguing a lot recently. Sue feels resentful that Tom has managed to keep working and feels he doesn't understand how hard it is for her in the day. Tom feels his job is also quite stressful and that it is hard to come home because he also feels a bit inadequate around Ben who clearly prefers to be with Sue.

After a particularly stressful week, Sue becomes very upset and tearful when Ben won't settle at bedtime, and angrily blames Tom for not helping her and accuses him of not doing his share and preventing her from going back to work. Tom waits until after the children have gone to bed, and suggests they need to find some time to be together and talk about what is going wrong. They arrange a time to have an evening in together and get a takeaway, and each takes it in turns to talk about what they are feeling frustrated about, and each agrees on one thing they can do to help the other. Tom agrees that he can spend a bit more time with Ben, getting more familiar with his routines and medical treatment, which will give Sue a break and help get Ben to trust him a bit more. Sue agrees that she will be more open with Tom about when she is feeling angry with him, rather than bottling it up. They will also spend some time talking together about how they are balancing work and home time, to see if there is a way of reducing stress for both of them.

When you are caught up in these cycles of resentment with your partner, the following strategies can helpful:

Take a step back

Difficult though it can be to 'step back' in these situations, it is important to try and find a way out of this cycle of resentment and perceived lack of support for each other. Someone has to take the first step, so try and be the one to take the initiative by suggesting you need to find some time to resolve your differences. Pick a moment when you are able to be calm and when your partner is most likely to be able to listen to your suggestions.

Straight talking

It is helpful to do some 'straight talking' – ask directly for what you want, rather than indirectly getting cross about what your partner hasn't done. Don't make assumptions about what your partner is thinking and don't let resentments build up. It is all too easy to feel dissatisfied and to blame your partner even when you have not directly communicated what you need. No one can read your mind, so try saying it as clearly as possible. And remember to encourage them to tell you directly what it is that is making them so angry with you and to suggest what you can do to help improve the situation.

For example, rather than saying, 'You're late – I've already done their bath!' say what you really mean, which might be, 'Please can you take over now and read the children a story and get them ready for bed.'

If you are angry about something, it is usually more productive to wait for a calmer time to talk about it. For example, you may be really annoyed your partner is late home, but better to ask directly for the help you need now, and later on talk about how to manage when he or she returns late. For example, 'I know you are sometimes held up at work, but please can you let me know so I can plan – otherwise I get annoyed because I was expecting you back by 6.30 and hoping for a break.'

Build in some time for yourselves

If you establish some 'couple time' right at the beginning when your baby is first born, this will become part of your normal routine. Many parents find it helpful to plan 'date nights' when they have some time for themselves as adults rather than just as parents or carers. It may be more difficult to find babysitters if your child is not well, which can make it hard to go out, but you can still plan to spend some time one evening a week catching up and enjoying adult conversation.

Key Points

- Caring can be very rewarding but also very stressful.

- Practical difficulties can also make it harder emotionally.

- You need to take care of yourself in order to manage caring for your child.

- Give yourself regular small treats – if you can, do something physical and social because this can help with making you feel more positive.

- Seek additional support if you need it.

- Set up ways of nurturing your relationships from the very beginning – it is easy for resentments to build up under stress and it is better to communicate and find out what you are both really thinking.

Resources

General Information and Specific Medical Conditions

Many of the websites set up to provide information and support for children and families affected by specific medical conditions have excellent resources. It is not possible to list every website, but examples include:

www.asthma.org.uk

www.cysticfibrosis.org.uk

www.diabetes.org.uk

You can usually find the charity or patient support group for your child's condition by putting the name of their condition into a search engine. There is sometimes more than one website or charity for a particular condition, so to find all the relevant patient support websites you can use the search function on the Contact website, the charity for families with disabled children, which will list the main sources of support for that specific condition:

www.contact.org.uk

There are also some general websites which address some of the issues covered in this book.

Financial and Practical Support

Your local authority will provide social care services for children and families, and if you want advice about financial and practical support you can also contact your local Citizens Advice Bureau:

www.citizensadvice.org.uk

There are charities that provide support for children with life-limiting or life-threatening conditions, including:

www.clicsargent.org.uk

www.rainbowtrust.org.uk

Psychological Wellbeing and Mental Health Difficulties

These websites provide information and support for children with psychological difficulties and their families – they may be helpful in understanding difficulties your child is having and also provide guidance about how to access further help if necessary:

www.childline.org.uk

www.minded.org.uk

www.place2be.org.uk

www.youngminds.org.uk

Resilience

This website describes an approach to developing resilience in children in order to help them rise above difficult circumstances and thrive, which is particularly appropriate for children and young people with long-term health conditions:

www.fosteringresilience.com

Helping to Prepare Your Child and Yourself for Hospital and Information about Hospital Procedures

There are some websites which provide general information as well as videos or pictures of medical procedures including CT and MRI scans, and ECG tests, etc. It can be very helpful to look through these first yourself, and then to show them to your child to help prepare them for their admission:

www.whatwhychildreninhospital.org.uk

The website for Great Ormond Street Hospital:

www.gosh.nhs.uk

Bereavement and Loss

There are several websites that provide information and resources for families and professionals when a child is near or at the end of life, including information about how to talk about death and dying to children and where to access support following bereavement. Some of the websites for specific conditions will contain useful information as well. The Children's Cancer and Leukaemia group – www.cclg.org.uk – produce an excellent booklet, *Facing the Death of Your Child*, which is free to download and is appropriate for other medical conditions, too. It also contains a useful list of books and resources for children and young people to help them understand about death and bereavement:

www.childbereavementuk.org

www.hospiceuk.org

www.togetherforshortlives.org.uk

www.winstonswish.org.uk

A telephone support line for support following the death of a child is run by the Child Death Helpline:

www.childdeathhelpline.org.uk

Managing Difference

These websites provide support for children with visible differences including strategies for building a child's self-confidence and managing teasing or bullying. Some excellent resources are also available on the websites for support groups and charities for conditions that affect appearance (e.g., www.eczema.org):

www.bullying.co.uk

www.changingfaces.org.uk

www.kidscape.org.uk

Schools

Many of the condition-specific websites provide information packs or guides for schools to help teachers understand and support children affected by a health condition. They also often suggest activities that can be done by teachers to help other children in the classroom understand the impact of the condition as well as promote positive attitudes towards managing difference.

The following websites provide information about the support for children with Special Educational Needs in school:

www.gov.uk/children-with-special-educational-needs

www.councilfordisabledchildren.org.uk/information-advice-and-support-services-network

www.gov.uk/governmentpublicationssupporting-pupils-at-school-with-medical-conditions--3

Siblings

Sibling charities and support via the Contact website or specific condition websites:

www.childrenssociety.org.uk/youngcarer/home

www.contact.org.uk

www.place2be.org.uk

www.sibs.org.uk

Adolescent Brain Changes

TED talk by Sarah-Jayne Blakemore: 'The mysterious workings of the adolescent brain':

https://www.ted.com/talks/sarah_jayne_blakemore_the_mysterious_workings_of_the_adolescent_brain

Caring for Yourself

This website provides both practical and emotional support for carers, including advice about eligibility for financial support and local resources:

www.carersuk.org

Relate provide counselling for relationship difficulties via a network of local counsellors with specific training in relationship counselling. They will also provide support for individuals and families as well as for couples:

www.relate.org.uk

There are now plenty of websites and apps for learning mindfulness techniques. Some of the most popular ones are listed here and you can listen to a sample first in order to find the best approach for you:

www.calm.com

www.headspace.com

www.stopbreathethink.com

You can refer yourself to your local IAPT (Improving Access to Psychological Therapy) service for help with managing anxiety, stress, depression or other mental health difficulties. To find your local service, you can use the search function on the NHS choices website:

www.nhs.uk

Index